Getting the Liturgy Right

Publications of the Joint Liturgical Group
established in 1963

The Renewal of Worship
The Calendar and Lectionary (1967, OUP)
The Daily Office (1968)
  10th corrected impression (1973, SPCK and Epworth)
An Additional Lectionary (1969, SPCK and Epworth)
Holy Week Services (1971, SPCK and Epworth)
Initiation and Eucharist (1972, SPCK)
Worship and the Child (1975, SPCK)
The Daily Office Revised (1978, SPCK)
Getting the Liturgy Right (1982, SPCK)

Getting the Liturgy Right

✠

*Essays by the Joint Liturgical Group
on Practical Liturgical Principles
for Today*

edited by
R. C. D. Jasper

LONDON
SPCK

First published 1982
SPCK
Holy Trinity Church
Marylebone Road
London NW1 4DU

ACKNOWLEDGEMENTS

Unless otherwise stated, the Scripture quotations in this publication are from the Revised Standard Version of the Bible, copyrighted 1946 and 1952 by the Division of Christian Education of the National Council of the Churches of Christ in the USA.

Printed in Great Britain by
Ebenezer Baylis and Son Ltd
The Trinity Press
Worcester and London

ISBN 0 281 03841 4

Contents

Statement of 11 October 1963

Informal discussions on liturgical matters between interested people from various Churches in Great Britain have indicated that the time is now ripe for the creation of a Joint Liturgical Group which can develop projects and questions of public worship. The Archbishop of Canterbury was asked to bring such a Group into being by issuing invitations to the Churches concerned to appoint members. His Grace kindly agreed to do so and himself appointed the representatives of the Church of England, while those of other Churches have been appointed by their respective bodies.

At its first meeting on 10–11 October 1963 the Group elected the Dean of Bristol as its Chairman and Dr Jasper as its Secretary.

It is clearly to be understood that any work produced by this Group will have no authority greater than that which its own members give to it by their own weight; but it will be for particular Churches, through their customary modes of decision, to make use of the results if they are willing to do so.

The initial projects which the Group has decided to discuss are these:

1 The planning of a Calendar, Forms of Daily Service, and a Lectionary which the Churches might be glad to have in common.
2 The planning of joint forms of service which might be used with the approval of the several Churches on occasions for united worship, such as the Week of Prayer for Unity and Holy Week.
3 The consideration of the structure of the service of Holy Communion.

Members of the Joint Liturgical Group

The Church of England
The Rev. D. C. Gray
The Very Rev. R. C. D. Jasper

The Church of Scotland
The Rev. D. M. Beckett
The Rev. J. C. Stewart

The Baptist Union of Great Britain and Ireland
The Rev. N. Clark
The Rev. M. F. Williams

The United Reformed Church
The Rev. D. McIlhagga
The Rev. Dr C. Thompson

The Methodist Church
The Rev. A. Raymond George
The Rev. Gordon S. Wakefield

The Churches of Christ
The Rev. Dr W. G. Baker

The Roman Catholic Church
The Rev. E. Matthews
The Rev. H. E. Winstone

1

Getting the Liturgy Right Practical Liturgical Principles for Today

☩

Donald Gray and Gordon Wakefield

'The gathering together of God's people in loving, adoring worship is the most expressive manifestation on earth – a veritable "epiphany" – of the Church; it betokens and reveals the Church.' So writes A. G. Martimort in *L'Eglise en Prière*.

Put in secular terms, worship is the most important of the Church's exercises in public relations. Yet it is directed towards God, not men, and is our response to his initiative in Christ. This is true of all the activities of worship, prayer, praise or penitence, and we must never for one moment forget it. But worship is proclamation of what is believed to be gospel, 'good news', and in our western world the Church is not a secret society, its mysteries hidden from all save the committed. This was so in the early Church when the catechumens left before the Lord's Prayer. But, with us, worship is public and anyone may enter the church and observe.

It is not unfair, and may help us in examining worship, if we ask what would a perfect stranger make of it all? What would he think our God was like, what would he consider to be his pre-occupations, and what would he assume were the type of people that these 'people of God' were aspiring to be?

He would judge far more by the 'spirit' and atmosphere than by any forms of words or rituals. Only if there was a sense of boredom, weariness, depression among the people would he complain about archaism or irrelevance, though he might express astonishment that tales from primitive tribes or banal

1

ditties or medieval costume could be the vehicles of such fervour and such obvious love. But if the people were participating with manifest joy and interest he could not dismiss the whole activity as valueless.

This 'spirit' is not something which a Worship Committee or a Parochial Church Council can create by democratic processes and a well-devised agenda. But it can take corporate possession if the people love each other and are longing to love God.

The old words of Cranmer's 1552 Eucharist disclose its secret, though perhaps they miss something of its rapture:

> Ye that do truly and earnestly repent you of your sins and are in love and charity with your neighbours and intend to lead a new life [rather *the* new life], following the commandments of God and walking from henceforth in his holy ways, draw near with faith . . .

Everything is secondary to that.

But if our stranger, dropping in, were sophisticated and intellectually aware, he would go on to assess the content of worship – the words, the music, the architectural setting, the gesture, vesture and posture. And if he came again, and again, he would expect that the set forms would bear constant repetition, that there would always be a certain freshness as well as a stabilizing invariability, and behind it all, something like a coherent philosophy of life.

We have to admit that he would find much to dishearten him in many congregations, much that would seem to have little connection with his daily life or the world of the news, much that presupposes a pre-scientific age and a rural, not industrial or urban society, its images and ideas at best quaint, at worst unintelligible when not repulsive.

We hope that these essays will help both clergy and laity to consider from first principles the mode, manner and presentation of their liturgy. It has been produced ecumenically because there is no basic disagreement between the major Christian confessions as to what worship should be either in its shape or essential elements. We have long since passed the point when denominational pride will prevent us using with full and open acknowledgement the accumulated wisdom of our fellow-Christians of traditions different from our own. In some cases we may learn from each other when a particular denomination by trial and experiment has found a solution which 'works'; at other times, we may unblushingly take over what belongs clearly to a well-tried tradition.

But when discussing the principles of worship, we need to keep certain points in mind:

1 In our world, we are all neighbours, but we are not all contemporaries. Some years ago, there was much tilting at 'the language of Canaan'. Twentieth-century man, so it was said, does not understand biblical and theological terms, and we have already conceded that our imaginary observer might condemn worship for its archaism. Yet in recent times there has been a revival of 'enthusiasm' which expresses itself quite uncritically in pietistic clichés and scriptural images. Nor is it without significance that in Africa and the Far East there is an increase of Christian allegiance that contrasts with the malaise of many Western Churches and would seem to validate the longer ending of St Mark's Gospel. This is no answer to the scepticism of scientific man, nor proof that Christianity can survive in a culture dominated by technology and empirical method. But it means that any group of people discussing worship may represent differences of historical period as well as of age, educational background and Christian experience.

2 Worship is a sensitive plant and its roots are in the soul. Disturb it, and it bleeds and weeps, for it belongs to the depths of being, to folk-memory, to childhood and our mother's knee, to our earliest aspirations and our need for security at last, far more than to the conscious activity of the discursive reason. That is why great delicacy is needed in liturgical discussion, for we are dealing with 'the stuff of life' as well as with the things of God. For this very reason we cannot allow bad theology in forms, which may in fact deny the gospel, to be passed on. (Cf. Erik Routley, *Church Music and Theology*.) But we must undertake our task with reverence and prayer.

3 A committee can no more devise living worship than build a tree. The Edwardine Prayer Books were issued under the imprimatur of a committee, but E. C. Ratcliff has argued cogently that this committee would merely accept what the chairman (Cranmer) set before it.[1] Some prayers – like those under the name of Michel Quoist – have been hammered out in groups,

and criticism and revision may be so undertaken. But this is not the way of artistic creativity. For the principal services, a worship committee will have before it the authorized denominational forms, which, these days, permit considerable freedom of choice in the Roman, Anglican and Church of Scotland rites. For less formal services, there is a wealth of material, old and new. But there may be someone in the company who has a real gift in the composition of prayers. And this should be encouraged.

4 The priest or minister has a distinctive role, but it will often be as guardian of the tradition and as a 'resource person' rather than as controlling voice. This is hard for him because nearly all our traditions have assumed that his was the last word in liturgical matters, that his predilections and preferences must be the ultimate arbiters. Nowadays, it is not even certain that he will be the most knowledgeable member of the group, liturgically or in anything else, though it is to be expected that he will have had the most training in ways of worship, and should have a particular and professional sensitivity which gives him an especial right to be heard, though this cannot always be taken for granted. And he ought to be the Greatheart of a pilgrim people. But the clergyman must learn that, without prejudice to his high privilege of being called to preside at the eucharistic assembly, worship belongs to the whole people of God.

5 The test of language and of all means of communication is far more than intelligibility. It is almost as important to give attention to music and movement, to colour and light, even to dress, as to words. Worship must be seen as a total activity. Yet there must be no theatrical self-consciousness and all must be under the control of *the* Word, who is Christ with his gospel in his Church. Rehearsal should not be disparaged. Forms of worship cannot be tested around a vestry table. And it is most necessary that the words of the prayers should be read aloud. This exposes the inadequacy, the chattiness, the verbosity of some of our contemporary compositions, even as it justifies those characteristics of Cranmer, tautologies and the like, which we despise as we sit at a desk or analyse in a seminar, but which become immediately vindicated when we remember that liturgy is to be declaimed both by president and people.

Liturgical revision could be the self-indulgence of antiquarians and aesthetes. Or it could be a game, the sophisticated 'Scrabble' of the ecclesiastical followers of King Canute – a word game in which the letters are shuffled around, but they are always the same letters, always the same board (bored?). Or it could be a real attempt to make the worship of Almighty God a 'veritable epiphany of the Church' and of the Church's Lord.

The supreme criterion is that worship must be authentically evangelical and catholic. It must reconstitute the crisis of the Church's origins, even when children are present, and proclaim the mystery of our communion with a Crucified and Risen Saviour.

NOTES

1 E. C. Ratcliff, *Liturgical Studies* (ed. A. H. Couratin and D. H. Tripp), 1976, p. 184.

2
Ministry

Harold Winstone and Edward Matthews

The Parish Church of St James in Gerrards Cross welcomes its visitors with the following notice to be found in every bench:

> If you are a newcomer to Gerrards Cross, will you treat this as a personal welcome to you from its vicar and people. We invite you to be part of the life and worship of our church. We offer you the happiness and friendship of this community, and we hope that you will discover for yourself the inspiration and help which means so much to us here.

What we are being offered is the church's *diakonia*, its ministry.

Ministry in the Early Church

It is strange how this word changed its meaning over the centuries. Originally it meant any and every service rendered by the Christian community, the servant Church, in fulfilment of its life and mission. Paul said (1 Cor. 12.5) 'There are varieties of service, but the same Lord.' He instanced the utterance of wisdom and knowledge, gifts of healing, the working of miracles, prophecy, discernment, tongues. These *charisms*, as they were called, were part of *diakonia*, ministry. In addition the New Testament mentions specifically apostles, pastors, presidents, prophets, evangelists, teachers and guardians as persons who exercise a *diakonia*. Nowadays when we talk of ministry we tend to think almost exclusively of the clergy, the official (ordained) 'ministers' of the Church, as though the whole of the Church's ministry were in their hands. The clergy are the ministers, the laity are those to whom they minister. A distinction of roles based on this premise, however, is entirely false and has done much to distort the average person's view of the Church.

A Concept of Ministry based on the Nature of the Church

The Christian community, i.e. the visible Church, is unlike any other kind of community in this respect, that the spirit which is its bond of unity is not an abstraction, like the need for protection or a shared interest, but the Spirit of the living God. The Church is alive with the Spirit. It shares the divine life. The Spirit that raised Jesus to life has entered the humanity with which Christ identifies, which is born again in him and which is now the living instrument of his activity in the world. In the Spirit *Christ* is now alive in his Church and works through it. The Church is therefore a living organism. In the blunt and very powerful language of Paul, it is the Body of Christ.

If this vital imagery is taken to its logical conclusion, then there are as many ministries in the Church as there are members. Every part of the body – as Paul insisted – ministers to the whole body and acts on behalf of the whole body (1 Cor. 12.12–31). No Christian is dispensable. Each is different and each has his or her part to play in the life and work of the Church. And this part is by no means an insignificant one. The whole Church indeed is a royal priesthood (1 Pet. 2.9; Rev. 1.6). By belonging to the Church the Christian is committed to everything that it exists for. Let us examine some of the more obvious things the Church exists for.

(*a*) *Preaching the Word*. No Christian is exempt from this duty. He belongs to a Church which exists to preach the Word. So when the Holy Spirit came on the Church at Pentecost, 'they were *all* filled with the Holy Spirit and preached the Word of God with boldness' (Acts 4.31). Paul wrote to the Christians in Rome: 'I am satisfied about you, my brethren, that you yourselves are full of goodness, filled with all knowledge, and able to instruct one another' (Rom. 15.14). And John wrote: 'The anointing which you have received from him abides in you, and you have no need that anyone should teach *you*; as his anointing teaches you everything' (1 John 2.27).

(*b*) *Pastoral Care*. Here again, it is the whole Church that is involved. To the Thessalonians Paul writes:

> We exhort you, brethren, admonish the idle, encourage the faint-hearted, help the weak, be patient with them all. See that none of you repays evil for evil, but always seek to do good to one another and to all. Rejoice always, pray constantly, give thanks in all circumstances; for this is the will of God in Christ Jesus for you. Do not quench the Spirit, do not despise prophesying, but test everything; hold fast what is good, abstain from every form of evil (1 Thess. 5.14–22).

(*c*) *Worship*. The liturgy of the Church is not a liturgy for a cultic caste, it is the liturgy of the whole people of God. The whole Church assembles for 'the breaking of bread' (1 Cor. 11.17–24), and each person brings to it and expresses in it something of himself.

One might also notice in passing the part that all members of the New Testament Church took in *Church Order*. The passage in Matthew 18.15–18 is generally considered by scholars to refer to this. 'If your brother sins against you, go and tell him his fault, between you and him alone . . . If he does not listen, take one or two others along with you, that every word may be confirmed by the evidence of two or three witnesses. If he refuses to listen to them, tell the church . . .' There is a frightening passage in Corinthians which confirms this involvement of the whole community in Church Order. Paul condemns the incestuous man and says to the Corinthian Christians: 'When you are assembled, and my spirit is present with the power of our Lord Jesus Christ, you are to deliver this man to Satan for the destruction of the flesh, that his spirit may be saved in the day of the Lord Jesus' (1 Cor. 5.4).

Official Ministries

From all that has been said so far one must not conclude that there was no official ministry in the New Testament. There clearly was. The choosing of the Twelve and the special commission Christ gave them is evidence of this. It is also clear that the Twelve appointed others. They appointed presidents for the communities to act in their place. Paul begins his letter to the Philippians with the words 'To all the saints in Christ Jesus who are at Philippi, with the bishops and deacons. . . .' (Phil. 1.1). They must feed the flock of which the Holy Spirit has made them overseers (Acts 20.28). Anyone who aspires to the office of bishop (overseer) desires a noble task (1 Tim. 5.17). We hear also of elders or presbyters. The terms 'bishop' and 'presbyter' could be applied to the same men or to men with identical or very similar functions. (Cf. ARCIC Canterbury Statement, section 6.) Those who ruled well, said Paul, were worthy of double honour, especially those who laboured in preaching and teaching (1 Tim. 4.17). The community owed them a living (1 Cor. 9.14). They were specially charged with looking after the sick (Jas. 5.14). Men were also appointed to assist the Twelve in the charitable work of the community (Acts 6.2–4). This may have given rise to the distinct order of deacons (servants). They had to be men of prayer who were filled with the Holy Spirit.

And so we trace the beginnings of an official ministry in the Church. It was an enabling ministry. It made it possible for the Church to function in the world in accordance with its purpose: i.e. to exercise its universal priesthood – preaching, baptizing, reconciling. Though a number of such ministries are named in the New Testament, eventually a threefold order emerged: bishops, presbyters and deacons. In the course of time the bishops and presbyters were regarded as belonging to a priesthood which resided primarily in the bishops and secondarily in the presbyters, who came to be called priests.

An official ministry that recognizes its role of service to the community is of great benefit to the Church, but problems arise when it acts independently of the community. It is then that we get the split between the teaching and the learning Church, the shepherds and the sheep. The Fathers of the Church were at pains to counter this. John Chrysostom wrote: 'The Eucharist is common to all. It is not just celebrated by the priest, but by the people with him. He begins only after the faithful have given their consent by proclaiming "It is right and fitting" ' (Hom. on 2 Cor. 18.3). In the *City of God* Augustine writes: 'We call all Christians priests because they are members of the one priest, Christ.' And again, in his commentary on the Petrine text, Matthew 16.18, he writes: 'You bind, too; and you loose . . . When the sinner is reconciled he is loosed by you, because you too pray to God for him.'

Possibly the Fathers had to labour these points because by the beginning of the fifth century it was not all that clear that the ministry was a service which enabled the servant Church to live out its priestly role in the world. One of the troubles was that the notion of *diakonia* was shrinking. What had once been a profusion of ministries was gradually becoming the preserve of a three-tier, and eventually a two-tier, ministry. In fact, by the time of the Reformation the ordained priesthood had more or less taken into itself all the other ministries, including those of later origin: acolytes, lectors, exorcists and door-keepers.

The Traditional Ministries

The Bishop and the Presbyter

To fulfil its mission and purpose the Church needs leaders. The Church is the community of those who have been called together through faith in the Word of God. It needs therefore leaders who can speak that Word, a Word of grace and redemption which builds up the Church, the Body of Christ. Furthermore, the Church is realized most concretely when it assembles to celebrate the Eucharist, and some leader is needed to preside.

The bishop (over a wide area) or the priest (usually in a local congregation) exercises this leadership. At the eucharistic assembly, in the name of the community and with the authority of Christ present in the community, he takes his natural place as president of the sacrament of unity, by which we receive the eucharistic Body and Blood of Christ. He does not, however, act independently of the community, for to have its full effect the eucharistic assembly must represent fully the daily life of the community. Liturgy is not, so to say, a sacred excrescence on life; it is the transformation of life, the authentic life of Christians. Hence, the person who presides at the Eucharist should be the person who presides in the life of the community, serving it not as though he were the sole recipient of divine wisdom, nor as one in authority whose word is law, but as president, orchestrator, one who can inspire others to give of their best in the service of the community, who can discern and encourage their particular charisms and enable them to be exercised, not stifled. That is, he must give real Christian leadership. It is a task which involves the whole man, and he need have no fears that anyone is going to take it away from him.

Once this view has been accepted, the way is once more open for other forms of *diakonia* in the Church. These must correspond to the real needs of the Church – that is to say, they must enable the Church to do its work in the world of today.

The specific mission of the Church is, as Paul says, to reconcile. 'It was God who reconciled us to himself through Christ and gave us this work of handing on this reconciliation' (2 Cor. 5.18–19). Crucial in this process is the Word which must be proclaimed (1 Cor. 1.7) and heard (Rom. 10.14). Hence in Christian tradition, ministry is regarded as having to do with 'leadership in creating channels of communication for the building up of a community covenanted and Spirit-filled in Christ Jesus'.[1]

The Diaconate
The deacon, originally ordained for the service of those in need, became the personal assistant of the bishop or priest in his work for the community. He preached, catechized, organized the community of prayer, baptized, distributed Communion, and officiated at weddings and funerals. In the Roman Catholic tradition the diaconate became a stepping-stone towards the priesthood, but it is recognized today that this is a ministry in its own right, and more and more married and single men are being ordained specifically to this ministry. Other traditions have been more ready to accept the service of a deaconess. There were deaconesses in the early Church, for example, Sister Phoebe (Rom. 16.1). One of their chief duties was to help at the baptism of women. In the Didascalia (Syria, mid-third century) we read 'You must honour the deaconess as the image of the Holy Spirit'.

The 'Minor' Orders
Until recently in the Roman Church there were four so-called 'minor' orders: exorcist, acolyte, door-keeper and lector. Let us consider first the *exorcist* – a hazardous ministry by all accounts. Exorcism was a part – though perhaps the most spectacular part – of the Church's healing ministry. Jesus was the great healer – not just of bodies but of the whole man ('Your faith has made you *whole*') – and he instanced healing as a visible sign of discipleship: 'In my name they will cast out devils, they will lay their hands on the sick.' The notion of exorcism, therefore, needs to be extended to include the caring ministry of the

11

Church. The special ministry of the Church is not social work as such – nursing, feeding the hungry, or any of the other corporal works of mercy – but being a channel of grace and divine reconciliation to people in their need. This is why the State cannot take over the role of the Church. To succour bodily need but to bring no healing to the spirit is to leave the human condition radically unchanged. The corporal and the spiritual works of mercy belong together. We need this visible ministry of the Church among our Christian doctors and nurses. What does it mean otherwise to be a *Christian* doctor?

We turn next to the *acolyte*: one who expresses by word and gesture the poetry of worship in the assembly. In many places his ministry has passed to the altar-servers, but it is an important ministry and much thought needs to be given to its proper exercise.

The '*door-keeper*' – perhaps sacristan – was the person who tolled the bell for worship and prayer, and welcomed the community into the house of God. There are many people who do this service, but often without much official recognition. It is a vital service and extends to making sure that everyone is made to feel at home in the church and is not ignored or 'left out in the cold'.

The *lector*, or reader, is one who has studied the scriptures and lives them, and has learned to proclaim the message with intelligence and sensitivity.

Ministries in Churches of the Reformation

Whereas the Roman Catholic Church still retains the traditional ministries which we have described, other forms and concepts of ministry developed in the Churches which were influenced by the Reformation.

The Anglican Church retained the traditional threefold ministry. It does not, however, have the 'minor orders'. It has, however, 'readers' who are authorized to conduct certain parts of public worship.

The Church of Scotland and the English Free Churches reverted to a single ministry of word and sacrament, which they regard as a return to the 'presbyter-bishops' of the New Testament. They believe in the parity of the ministry; their 'presidents', 'moderators', 'chairmen', 'superintendents' and so on claim to exercise no higher ministry than other ordained ministers. Oversight (*episcope*) of ministers and churches is exercise by church courts. Some of them have also elders who, although laymen (at least in the popular sense of that word), are ordained to help in the pastoral work of the Church. Some of them have deacons, who, unlike Roman Catholic or Anglican deacons, are laypeople, and who help in the administrative work of the Church. Elders and deacons often assist the ministers in the administration of Holy Communion. Most of them have readers or lay preachers.

The Methodist ministry has its own special history. John Wesley gathered a body of preachers who were mostly laymen. They were divided into travelling preachers in full connexion with the Methodist Conference and local preachers. In the course of time the custom arose of ordaining the travelling preachers in full connexion. The local preachers conduct many of the preaching-services. There are no elders or deacons, but lay leaders and pastoral visitors do much of the pastoral work and stewards do much of the administrative work.

The Church of Scotland and some of the English Free Churches have various ways of describing those who are exercising some ministerial functions in preparation for the ordained ministry (just as Roman Catholic and Anglican deacons are often, though not necessarily, preparing for the priesthood). Thus, for example, the Church of Scotland licenses them as preachers of the gospel and probationers for the holy ministry. In Methodism also those who are historically travelling preachers on trial and not yet in full connexion are now known as probationers.

Nearly all of these Churches, including the Anglican Churches, have deaconesses, who, whether ordained or commissioned, are usually regarded as laywomen. In all these Churches it is usually an ordained minister who presides at the Lord's Supper, but some of them, regarding it simply as a matter of order, sometimes exercise the right for due reason to authorize laypeople to preside.

Thus all of these Churches in various ways have that corporate concept of ministry which we have described, together with official ordained ministers, who exercise special functions of leadership in connection with preaching and the sacraments.

Other Ministries

Many other ministries come to mind: the church musician, the catechist, the spiritual counsellor or confessor, the youth counsellor and youth leader, the Christian social worker, the Sunday school teacher, the parish lay worker, and the lay missionary. Every Christian community has these people among its members, but because the idea of ministry has become so attenuated in the Church as a whole they do not often get the support and encouragement they need. They are not regarded as ministers at all. This is one of the reasons why the Church's pastoral work is so often amateurish and haphazard. Too few people are encouraged to devote themselves wholeheartedly to the development and deployment of their particular charism in the service of the Church. Because there are so few ministerial structures

(*a*) people with a particular bent do not know how to set about using it for the mission of the Church;

(*b*) they very often lack the support and encouragement of others engaged in the same ministry;

(*c*) the Church is not seen to be doing anything more than dabbling in a given area. Christian life in a community of faith, when lived to its fullest, requires a rich and recognizable diversity of ministerial witness to remain authentic to itself in its mission to the world. [2]

By creating an official ministry the Church commits itself to the viability of that ministry. As we have seen, many people do a service in the community of the Church without receiving any official recognition by the community. They do a Christian work but in their own right as baptized Christians, not in the name of the community. This means that the community as such does not make itself responsible for the viability of this work. Even projects organized at parochial level sometimes suffer from this disability. The 'minister' asks for helpers in the parish or local church (organists, choristers, catechists, social workers) but very little is done by way of training these people to do their work efficiently, and the parish or local church as such does not feel any great involvement. Nor do the workers themselves recognize any special mandate from the community. The advantage of an official ministry is that it gives official recognition to the gifts that God has given his people, and everyone can appreciate more fully how these gifts contribute to the building up of the Body of Christ.

Everything that the Christian community does through its individual members should be seen as the work of the whole community and should receive the blessing and support of the whole community. That is what constitutes ministry. The form in which this blessing and support is given is of great importance because it affects the Church's awareness of itself and of its mission. In the early Church the community commissioned its ministers through prayer and the laying-on of hands. This sacramental action might well be revived generally in the Church. Probably what is needed is a formula of commissioning that can become recognized by Christians throughout the world.

QUESTIONS FOR DISCUSSION

1 'I would like to thank the parish priest and his people for supporting this charity.' Does anything strike you as odd about that statement? Compare it with Paul's mode of address in Phil. 1.1.

2 What does the phrase 'The Church teaches . . .' really mean?

3 Can you suggest kinds of ministries that are urgently needed in today's Church for it to fulfil its life and mission?

4 The local Church should have a say in the appointment of its ministers. Do you agree?

5 Compose a commissioning service for the institution of a parish catechist.

NOTES

1 Blenkinsopp, *Celibacy, Ministry, Church*, p. 121.
2 'Ministries in the Community and in the Liturgy,' *Concilium*, vol. 2,8, p. 64.

3
The Setting of Worship

✠

Donald Gray

'We don't need churches – you can worship God anywhere.' So it is asserted: and the Church has to have an answer ready. It will admit that there is much truth there; yet at the same time it will have to point to evidence of man's ineradicable desire to have special places (temples, churches, groves) in which to invoke the deity.

The Church nowadays faces criticism of its churches, chapels and cathedrals, and many a homesick backward glance is cast towards the homeliness of the earliest Christian worship. It is certainly true that in the first three hundred years of the Christian era there were no specifically church buildings, and Christians met for worship in the houses of the faithful. Why was this? J. G. Davies finds the answer in the words, poverty, paucity and persecution.[1] Christianity, that is to say, in its early history was a predominantly working class movement, meeting in small groups, with the possibility of persecution always around the corner. From the time of Constantine, when Christianity began to replace the pagan cults as the state religion, worship lost its domestic setting and became a public occasion. Buildings now had to match the Church's new-found status, and first the basilicas, then the great parish churches and cathedrals began to dominate the landscape of Christendom. There was no longer any need for secrecy; the age for proclamation had dawned.

Churches and cathedrals were built to the glory of God and had certain essential features. Chief of these was the altar, to which had to be given the highest dignity and honour. In the Middle Ages, alas, multiplication of chapels, each with its own altar, tended to obscure the centrality of the principal altar, but it was this focal point that gave the building its unique significance. Related to the altar were the episcopal throne, the ambo (pulpit) and the font, which was housed outside the early basilica in a separate baptistry.

Altar, throne and ambo

The early church buildings, then, had three focal points – the altar, the throne and the ambo, and all our church buildings today have these same features, even if we give them different names. Any congregation anxious to bring its liturgy alive is bound to be deeply concerned with the position of these same objects, and of the congregation in relation to them. In the past a decision on whether it would be the altar or the pulpit (ambo) which arrested the eye on entering the building depended upon the current state of theological opinion about the comparative importance of the Eucharist or the preaching of the Word. Today we want to emphasize that the two are complementary, and do not want to drive a wedge between them. To give each of these functions of the Christian Church an equal dignity of place seems to us to speak the message that it is equally in the breaking of the bread and in the 'dividing' of the Word that Christ is given. This conviction means that both in the planning of new churches as well as in the re-ordering of the old neither feature will dominate and both will be equally prominent.

Alongside this it will be necessary to consider the design of both the altar and the ambo. In some cases where a re-ordering is taking place there may be no need to replace the existing furniture. In others it may be thought that what has been inherited does not speak truly to an age which shrinks from ostentation. It has always to be remembered that the removal of old and familiar furniture is in any event a bitter pill for many worshippers to swallow.

In Roman Catholic churches the immediate visible outcome of Vatican II and the Constitution on the Sacred Liturgy was the provision of a freestanding altar 'in the face of the people'. The High Altar, the previous focus of attention, was now downgraded, and a more functional altar was introduced. At the same time, provision was made for the lections to be read with all due dignity at a lectern, thus emphasizing the distinc-

17

tive elements of word and sacrament which together comprise the Church's definitive act of worship – the Eucharist. Fears have been expressed that to separate the two places where the liturgy as a whole is performed will be to put asunder what is joined together. But as long as the two places of interest are seen to be related to each other, and there is not a positive shunning of the altar during the fore-mass (to the point almost of pretending it is not there) then what has been called 'the Bible class' can be seen as a proclamation and celebration of the word of God through the reading of the scriptures, entirely complementary to the gift of God which is shared under the signs of bread and wine.

There is another piece of furniture which can help to ensure that the eucharistic action as a whole is seen and understood. This is the presidential chair, which is a development from the episcopal throne. The president of the eucharistic assembly needs to be plainly seen to be presiding over the whole action, and should never disappear from view. His chair, therefore, should so be placed as to suggest that he is actively guiding the assembly in its worship. As president he should retain to himself, regardless of the parts played by the other clergy and ministers, the initial greeting of the congregation and the collect preceding the lections which is the prayer of the Church for that particular day or feast. The one presidential figure should be clearly in charge of any Eucharist from the beginning to the end without prejudice to the functions of deacons, readers, servers or interceders.

Place of Baptism

It has already been observed that the earliest purpose-built churches provided a separate baptistry. In the early church there was a strict discipline about concealing the sacred mysteries from the uninitiated. Those who were under instructions (catechumens) were allowed to be present only for the first part of the Eucharist. It was therefore not to be wondered at if baptism was not a public event and required a special room or even building in which the rite could be performed. However, as the population as a whole became nominally Christian, such precautions were unnecessary; nothing more was needed than the provision of a font within the church building, and this began to be the custom in the Western Church. There were a few years of debate, over the attempt by mother churches to retain their right to baptize rather than allowing baptisms to take place in dependent churches and chapels, but with this controversy out of the way we find that all churches were now furnished with a font. It was usually positioned at the west end of the church near the principal door, symbolizing that baptism is the 'door of all sacraments'. This had the effect that on entering church all were reminded that no one could enter the Church without initiation. The Liturgical Movement's influence on the setting for baptism was to revive the primitive idea of the baptistry. The importance of baptism ought to be given due emphasis, it was realized, and this should be expressed in the provision of a decent space suitable to the dignity of the sacrament. Present-day building costs entirely ruled out, of course, the supplying of a separate building or even room for baptisms; nor is this desirable if the point is taken that the initiation of adults or children into the church ought not to be a hole-in-the-corner affair on a Sunday afternoon, but an occasion at which the people of God would want to be present – present not only to witness but to welcome, and at the same time to be reminded of the high calling of their own baptism. This would mean the provision of a building large enough to accommodate the normal Sunday congregation – a second church! Alongside these considerations must be placed the new understanding of the interrelationship of the two gospel sacraments which has resulted in the adoption in some modern buildings of the Lutheran *Prinzipalstück* – a single space at the east end of a church in which all the principal liturgical acts are conducted and thus altar, font and pulpit are all brought together.

The Congregational Seating

Whatever conclusion we reach about the most suitable place for the furniture of the church, we must never forget that 'the Church is not a building: it is people'. The positioning of the people of God within the building, and their physical relationship with the liturgical furniture – and with each other – is even more important than the objects themselves.

Many congregations are no more than a cross-section of the

local community conveniently housed under one roof for an hour or so each week. The front pews remain empty and the rest of the seats are filled haphazardly.

A church with fixed pews presents a formidable prospect for a congregation wanting to express its corporateness and in many places a policy of reducing the number of pews could be pursued with immense advantage. Some churches hesitate to do this fearing that they betray a lack of confidence in the return of the days of faith, when people will flock back to church! If only they would study the statistics of the past and realize that memory plays tricks and that the actual number of times when there were 'chairs in the aisles' in the good old days were few and far between. What is probably remembered is the chapel anniversary, harvest festival or some such occasion, which was more a community gathering in the days when there were rare opportunities for a jamboree of any kind. Both church and state in the mid-nineteenth century, having worked out that there was a gap between the available number of church sittings and the increased populations, built innumerable churches for the masses to stay away from.

The number of seats a church requires is represented by its normal Sunday congregation. It is infinitely better to make special arrangements for the exceptional occasions than to have a permanent arrangement which makes it almost impossible to celebrate the Eucharist intelligently week by week. If there is a desire to impress the casual visitor on a special occasion, a leaf can perhaps be taken out of the book of the resourceful Dean F. W. Dwelly of Liverpool. He was said to have often given instructions for fewer chairs to be put out in the Cathedral for a specific occasion than were likely to be needed so that people went home saying 'It was marvellous – they even had to bring in extra chairs'.

The arrangement of the seating ought in itself to give a feeling of community. A semi-circle or even a circle of chairs with the altar 'in the round' can produce an atmosphere of corporateness which few other means can achieve. This points to the need for movable furniture whenever possible. Different occasions have different needs, so flexibility is the greatest need.

The Narthex

Some modern churches have been designed to include a gathering area, variously the Narthex or Galilee. Such an arrangement can help individuals to begin the process of becoming a congregation from the moment they arrive at church and it also prevents a hurried exit after the service, so that people can talk and meet together. The possibility of using this area for tea or coffee after the service has been widely grasped; but it provides many other possibilities for building-up the fellowship which has been proclaimed in the eucharistic assembly.

Symbolism in Liturgy

Human beings are symbol-making creatures, and signs and symbols have always occupied an important place in the Christian Church. This has been true quite apart from the varied interpretation or scale of significance that has been given to them. Although at various periods some symbols have been discarded while others were retained, yet 'there has rarely been any disposition to discount the necessity of, or to minimize the significance of symbols for the initiation and the development of the Christian life'. [2]

We can all get water nowadays by turning a tap, but we still value it no less for washing and for drinking. In the same way, although the loaf can be bought in quantity, sliced and wrapped, at the supermarket, the slightest whiff of a shortage causes widespread panic and visions of starvation. Here then are two symbols which still speak to us because they derive from experience common to us all.

We should beware of esoteric symbols which have no roots except in church tradition, and therefore are only appreciated by a small 'in-group', and serve to foster an image of the Church as a secret society. In authentic Christianity the only secret is that there is no secret! All is open to those who 'have ears to hear'. There are some who bemoan the loss of a sense of mystery in worship. If this can be induced only by dim lights and incomprehensible gestures, we must surely be well rid of it. What we can regret is some of the contemporary over-familiarity and casualness with the sacred and seeming lack of preparation for things of the spirit.

We must find ways to combine the best of the new with the best of the past, so that the great treasury of Christian sign and symbol can be open to all. On this matter the wisdom of the 1549 Prayer Book is unlikely to be bettered: 'as touching, kneeling, crossing, holding up of hands, knocking upon the breast and other gestures, they may be used or left, as every man's devotion serveth without blame.'

NOTES

1 J. G. Davies, *The Secular Use of Church Buildings*, 1968, p. 1.
2 F. W. Dillistone, *Christianity and Symbolism*, 1955.

4

The Bible and the Liturgy

✠

Neville Clark

In the house of liturgy the central place of Scripture is secure. Some occupants may be able to claim no more than squatters' rights and be in constant danger of eviction. Others may give the appearance of being guests whose departure might one day be envisaged. The Bible, however, belongs. There is indeed more than a suggestion that a substantial proportion of the liturgical mansion was specially designed for its accommodation. That Old and New Testaments should be read is a directive which would seem to many as unchallengeable as an entry in the title-deeds.

The fact is that the significant contemporary questions do not arise at this point. They stem rather from the fact that Scripture has not confined itself to the commanding position already suggested. There is an uneasy feeling to be reckoned with that the Bible, far from being content with its own magnificent liturgical quarters, has over the centuries laid claim to be the dominating presence throughout the whole house. This biblical imperialism is seen to characterize the main body of contemporary liturgical revision and to carry with it two fundamental weaknesses. On the one hand, legitimate cries for meaningful relevance go unheeded. On the other hand, the fruits of modern biblical understanding are at crucial points ignored.

Precisely at this point J. L. Houlden levels the indictment in reasonably representative fashion. 'It seems to be deemed sufficient to make liturgical forms virtually catenae of biblical words and images. To do that is to "use" the Bible. There has been little sign of any serious attempt to consider whether these words and images still carry their former vividness or are intelligible expressions of what is to be said. Nor is there much sign of awareness of the echoes and contexts of biblical allusions: the mere fact of allusion is sufficient.'[1] Granted that the specific target of the accusations is Rite A in the new Anglican *Alternative Service Book*, it may reasonably be supposed that similar comments might be levelled against the liturgy as performed in other traditions.

The charge is a serious one. It may serve as a reminder that the problem of the place of Scripture within the liturgy has scarcely begun to be solved responsibly when attention is concentrated simply on the provision of an adequate and ordered supply of biblical readings and a generous and pervasive sprinkling of the liturgy with scriptural reminiscences. The real issue is how Scripture functions and therefore how it is rightly used in the liturgical context. To get the liturgy right certainly involves the answering of a whole range of practical questions. What version(s) of the Bible is to be read? Should non-biblical literature find a place? How far should liturgical language and imagery be scriptural and how far severely contemporary? Should biblical content be a test of the adequacy of hymnody? Yet danger arises when such questions are answered without prior and careful attention to more basic issues related to the purpose and place of Scripture itself and without proper recognition that a coherent approach demands coherent perspectives.

Basic Perspectives

How then does the Bible function in the liturgical context? It does not act as a vehicle of direct theological instruction or concrete ethical directive. Rather does it operate as the primary instrument of Christian formation whereby the community of faith is placed under the Gospel and built into its Lord. Scripture is the Church's authoritative control. It enshrines the foundational story of God's creative and redemptive travail with his people, the strange fulfilment of that encounter, and its sovereign claim upon all creation. To 'hear the Word of God' is to be set afresh under the promise and the imperative of that foundational story and therefore to be set anew between remembrance and hope.

It is, however, just here that the call of meaningful relevance becomes strident. Is not Scripture essentially of the 'past' and therefore remote? Its imagery does not ring meaningfully in the ears of modern man. Its language is the very opposite of common coinage and is scarcely calculated to foster intelligible and fruitful trading in the contemporary market place. Certainly it must be given a proper and necessary place within the total liturgy; but its pervasive and exclusive claims must be resisted. It must indeed be 'put in its place', and even there be dressed in the most modern garb available. And, in the end, of what use is the biblical story if the congregation cannot liturgically table its own story in its own language with equal scope and weight?

To brush that plea aside would be indeed to be guilty of liturgical antiquarianism. To deal with it responsibly is, however, no easy matter. The very structure of the liturgy presses in the direction of one particular solution. There is the Proclamation of the Word of God. There is the subsequent Response to the Word of God. It is but a tiny step to a shorthand labelling of these two sections as Divine Address and Human Response. It is an even quicker step to a neat division of labour which sets manageable parameters for the place of Scripture in the liturgy. First the language and imagery of the past, then the language and imagery of the present. First the word from ancient times, then the contemporary expression of human experience. First the biblical story, then the congregation's own story. Even the order of priorities seems impeccable!

Yet to move in that direction would be to misconceive disastrously the nature and strategy of the biblical engagement with the contemporary congregation. The worshippers bring themselves, their lives and labours, their experience and world to the touchstone of Scripture so that a disturbing, transforming and redemptive encounter may be effected. The biblical story is laid upon the contemporary story, and no neat 'fit' is to be expected. For the Bible works in the liturgy to deepen formation into Christ, and such formation is never a smooth and painless process.

That is why it will not do to shut up Scripture within a segment of the liturgy and insulate contemporary experience and response from it. The Bible belongs on both sides of the liturgical equation. Scriptural story and congregational story must fuse. The sermon is classically and focally the point at which such

B

fusion is effected. Nevertheless, the biblical control rightly extends into the areas of prayer and hymnody. To pray (or praise) 'in the Spirit' is to pray (or praise) 'through Jesus Christ'. To pray 'through Jesus Christ' is to pray in conformity with the gospel. The road to that conformity runs inexorably through Scripture.

Issues for Decision

It is such basic perspectives that will determine the way in which a variety of practical issues require to be faced. In what version or versions is Scripture to be read? Were the basic aim an instructional one, then powerful arguments could be advanced to the effect that instant intelligibility should be the dominating, perhaps the only, criterion. If, however, the aim is Christian formation, then other standards will apply. Certainly obscurity, however hallowed and ancient, has nothing to commend it, and intelligibility remains a prize of considerable worth. Equally, the matter of suitability for public reading will be judged important. There will, however, be a special concern that the heights and depths of a time-laden and evocative imagery are not blithely sacrificed on the altar of the passing clichés of a flat linguistic modernity. From the same perspective, radical question marks will be placed against any tendency to use the plethora of available translations as a happy hunting ground for the 'best' rendering of each required reading. The Christian formation of the people of God is not best served by a stylistic mishmash.

Does the biblical literature have exclusive rights within the liturgy? Is there not a place for the use of other and later Christian writing? Does not the exclusion of such a potential treasury unwarrantably impoverish Christian worship? Do not the centuries provide us with a range of Christian literature that we may judge inspiring and profitable for the health of a congregation?

Such questions are not to be treated lightly. It is indeed arguable that (particularly in Churches that lack a prescribed liturgy) the baneful impression of the 'pastness' of Scripture has been accentuated by the fact that the only accompaniment to the biblical voice has tended to be the voice of the present moment. There has been comparatively little to remind the congregation of the centuries of tradition which link 'then' and 'now'.

Cranmer, Wesley and Watts may not be the only additional voices that could with profit be heard in the land.

Careful thought is, however, required as to the point at which and the way in which the wider range of Christian voices is allowed to sound. To weave them into the sermon may sometimes be the solution, though this will not always be either possible or appropriate, especially if the material in question is 'literary' and lengthy. The alternative is to recognize that later Christian literature is, in a real if indirect sense, commentary on Scripture and therefore to present it clearly and explicitly as such. What must be avoided is any special and solemn presentation that too easily suggests that a similar status to that belonging to Scripture is being accorded. From this perspective, it may appear that the really damaging aspect of an otherwise helpful recent compilation[2] in this field is in fact its title.

It remains to ask to what extent the total sweep of Scripture is properly usable within the liturgy. Must it not be admitted that for this purpose substantial parts of the Bible should be and are discarded? Is Leviticus the stuff of Christian formation? Are imprecatory psalms the staple diet of the worshipping people of God? Is not selectivity both praiseworthy and inevitable?

In some sense the psalms constitute a special case precisely because they are widely used for more than one liturgical purpose. They may be employed as material for Scripture readings. They may also be used as vehicles of responsive prayer and praise. *In the latter case*, it is entirely right that discriminating judgements be made as to whether certain portions of the Psalter can with integrity sound forth from the lips of a Christian congregation. It cannot be automatically assumed that a concluding Gloria infallibly sanctifies everything that precedes it.

Scripture, however, is more than psalmody. The wider question remains. It may appear that where a lectionary is used the verdict has already been rendered. For the modern lectionary operates on a principle of selectivity. It includes some biblical passages. *De facto* it excludes others. It offers a narrower canon than the inherited Bible. Is this defensible, and what are its implications?

Care is necessary at this point. A mechanistic use of

Scripture is unjustifiable. Each paragraph or chapter is not a unit of exactly equal weight with every other, nor does the absence of some sections necessarily distort the whole. Yet the road of selection remains a perilous path beset by a host of unbiblical spirits whose leaders are named Arbitrariness and Subjectivity, and probably no lectionary survives entirely unscathed.

'The primary aim is to let Scripture speak and impose its own terms.'[3] The search must be for a balance in selection that serves a wholeness of witness. It is not that every verse of Scripture must be read to a worshipping congregation. It is rather that, over a manageable period, the total witness of Scripture must be offered for the hearing. Nor is this all. The preacher must remember that the *total* canon of Scripture imposes itself for his plundering. And the congregation must recognize that the restricting of the use of Scripture to the confines of the liturgical assembly is the recipe for immaturity.

The Freedom of Biblical Control

Are we back then to a biblical imperialism? A plea of guilty must certainly be entered to the extent that the place of the Bible in the liturgy is not to be plotted in terms of a bounded segment marked 'Scripture Readings'. What must, however, be stressed is the *way* in which the Bible rightly pervades the liturgical celebration. Its function at this point is to act as an overarching control; and scriptural control is not the same thing as scriptural phraseology. The language of hymns and prayers, of praise and preaching, may with devastating accuracy and uniformity reproduce the biblical text, the biblical image, the biblical allusions. Yet the end result may be profoundly 'unbiblical'. Conversely, the language may contain little in the way of explicit biblical echo, yet the result may be 'biblical' through and through. The criterion is not verbal identity. It is something much more like what, in the context of translation, is termed 'dynamic equivalence'. What is spoken, sung, or proclaimed may and sometimes must be inescapably 'of our time', provided only that it springs from a deep biblical comprehension and manifests a deep subservience to scriptural control.

For to perform the liturgy is to re-enact the drama of

redemption of which the Bible provides the script. No congregation can rewrite that drama to suit its own taste or its own sense of what is relevant. It must faithfully speak the lines given to it. Yet this drama is above all one in which the disciplined actor is invited, encouraged and required to 'ad lib' to an almost unprecedented extent, and thereby to insert contemporary life and experience in all its range and reach. The only and the necessary proviso is that the 'ad libbing' shall not conflict with the dramatic movement but rather serve and enrich it.

NOTES

1   J. L. Houlden, *Explorations in Theology No. 3,* 1978, p. 89.
2   C. Campling, *The Fourth Lesson in the Daily Office*, 2 vols., 1973–4.
3   R. C. D. Jasper (ed.), *The Calendar and Lectionary*, 1967, p. 18.

5
The Preaching Content of Worship

✠

Harold Winstone

The Word in Worship

All Christian worship is grounded on the firm conviction that God has spoken to his people and still speaks to them. His word is recorded in the Scriptures and is communicated by being read prayerfully in private or proclaimed publicly in the Christian assembly. The basic attitude of the Christian is to be a listener: someone with open ears and an open heart. The attitude of the one who proclaims the word in the assembly is to be a servant of the word, to have read it carefully beforehand, to have assimilated it, and then to proclaim it with clarity and intelligence.

The way in which the word is proclaimed will vary according to circumstances and custom. There is an authentic type of Christian spirituality which reverences the word of God to such an extent that it is impatient of any slightest intrusion of the reader's personality. The word must not be 'subjectivized'. It must come across as the pure, objective word of God, not as a word that is interpreted and nuanced by the speaker. Hence in some traditions a mode of proclamation has been devised which ensures that the personality of the reader is subordinated as effectively as possible to the word. The Scriptures are 'monotoned', i.e. recited on one note, or chanted to an unvarying pattern of reciting-note and cadence.

On the other hand, the producers of televised religious services usually demand a style of proclamation which is much more akin to that of public speaking. The reader has a message to proclaim and he must be fully conversant with the techniques of public communication.

30

Between these two extremes are to be found varying styles of proclamation suiting different kinds of Christian assemblies. One factor, however, emerges clearly, whatever style of proclamation is chosen. It is that the reading from the Scriptures in Christian liturgy has a sacred character. It is a communication of the divine word and a celebration of God's presence to his people. It is therefore a work of the Holy Spirit who is the instigator of all Christian proclamation ('No one can confess "Jesus is Lord" unless he is guided by the Holy Spirit' – 1 Cor. 12.3). It is therefore the manifestation of a charism in the service of the community, and to that extent a special ministry.

The Relationship of Word to Sacrament

In the early days of the Church in Jerusalem Christians would attend the Temple services of readings, psalms and prayers, and then assemble in each other's houses for the breaking of bread (Acts 2.46). Later, when they were excluded from the Temple, a service of the word seems to have preceded the celebration of the Eucharist. This is certainly the most obvious inference to be drawn from the description in Acts of the Saturday evening 'fellowship meal' celebrated by Paul with the Christians of Troas when Eutychus went to sleep during the sermon and fell from the third storey window (Act 20.7–12).

This relationship of word to sacrament became traditional in Christian worship. All the Gospel accounts of Christ's feeding the people are preceded by a reference to his preaching. First he gave them God's word, then he fed them (Matt. 14.13–21); (Mark 6.34–6; Luke 9.10–17; John 6.1–14). In the Eucharist the sacramental communication of Christ to his people is preceded by the communication of his word. Both are a revelation of his presence among those who are gathered together in his name, and effectively bring about that presence. In the readings God speaks to his people of redemption and salvation and nourishes their spirits: 'the table of God's word is laid before the people' (General Instruction on the Roman Missal, para. 34). In the sacrament God 'keeps his word' and nourishes the people with the true bread from heaven.

The Sermon in the Eucharistic Assembly

Preaching is an integral part of the liturgy of the word and serves

31

the purpose of 'breaking the word' for the assimilation of a particular congregation. It serves to clarify the original meaning of the biblical text and relate it to the needs and concerns of the actual worshipping community. If it is to do this effectively the preacher needs to know not only the content of the Christian message, but also his audience.

The sermon serves also as a bridge between the two parts of the liturgy, the word and the sacrament, unifying them and bringing them together in one celebration. It is a vital part of the ongoing movement of the celebration which, beginning with the proclamation of the word, will culminate in the embodiment of that word in the community through its sacramental union with Christ in the Eucharist. Hence it should proclaim and make evident what God has accomplished in Christ and what he is doing in his people through the liturgy that is being celebrated on the particular occasion.

Scriptural Services

A liturgy of the word is not just the prelude to a eucharistic celebration, it is also a service in its own right. When Christians assemble for worship they come specifically to pray; and all Christian prayer is nourished by the word of God. It is a contemplation of that word, and issues in acts of praise, thanksgiving and intercession. In a non-eucharistic service the sermon will naturally form the high point for it is a communication of the divine message especially directed to the particular congregation and a response to the Lord's command to preach the gospel.

The Content of the Sermon

All Christian preaching is a proclamation of the good news. It is *kerygmatic* – a word derived from the Greek word for a herald. It 'proclaims to all people the wonderful things that the Lord has done' (Ps. 96). We see this exemplified in the sermons of the apostles recorded in the early chapters of Acts to which the people responded: 'We have heard them preach in our own language [i.e. in words we can understand] the marvellous works of God' (Acts 2.11). This style of preaching is particularly well suited to Christian liturgy, which is the celebration of what God in his great love has done and continues to do for us in Christ.

Within this framework there are a number of specific elements in traditional Christian preaching which deserve study. These elements can conveniently be listed under four headings: exegetical, catechetical, ethical and devotional. Some sermons may be predominantly characterized by one or other of these elements, but most sermons will contain a mixture of all four.

(*a*) *Exegetical*. The purpose of this element is to clarify and explain the original meaning of the sacred text and to apply it to the present situation. The Bible contains a great variety of literary genres. There is sacred history, allegory, drama, poetry, philosophy, ethics, prophecy, to mention but a few, and each of these forms of literature has its own characteristics and principles, a knowledge of which can help to clarify the precise meaning of a particular passage. Also one needs to know the historical, political and sociological background of the different writings, the terms of reference which the sacred author has set himself, his cast of mind and his purpose in writing. All this will throw a revealing light on the precise meaning of a particular passage. It is important to understand this if one is not to be trapped in a fundamentalist approach to the Scriptures which does no service either to the divine message or to the religious development of those to whom the message is addressed.

(*b*) *Catechetic*. The aim of this element is to instruct a congregation in the various doctrines of the Christian faith. The sermon may be predominantly apologetical, in the sense that it seeks to defend the faith in the face of contrary opinions (heresies), or simply explanatory, i.e. explaining in simple terms what the faith is and exploring some of the more relevant theological insights. The aim is to impart a more adult faith and a deeper understanding of the Christian mysteries (cf. *The Mystagogic Catecheses* attributed to Cyril of Jerusalem).

A currently popular form of catechetical preaching is the development of a theme, usually a biblical theme. The preacher takes as his starting-point one of the great Christian themes, such as covenant, salvation history, the kingdom, the second coming, and explores it with reference to present-day events and incidents in the daily experience of his hearers. The theme is usually one suggested by the readings for the day and can be illustrated by the prayers and other elements taken from the liturgy.

(*c*) *Ethical*. Here the aim is not so much instruction as an exhortation to the hearers to order their lives on the precepts of the gospel: to put the faith into action. A good example of this is provided by the Epistle of James. A modern equivalent would be the castigation of the evils of our twentieth-century society. In some Christian traditions the ethical sermon almost became the norm, but a moralizing or exhortatory element will be found in most sermons, if only in the peroration.

(*d*) *Devotional.* This is the preached meditation. It is a prayerful presentation of the word particularly well suited to worship in small groups or on the occasion of a spiritual retreat or day of recollection. It aims to evoke a prayerful response to God's word and is fittingly followed by a period of silent adoration and praise. In a tempestuous age of loud and ranting speeches, loud music, and every other kind of noise, a sermon of this kind can provide a haven of peace and recollection so essential to the deepening of the human spirit. 'With desolation is all the land made desolate because there is no one who considers in the heart' (Jer. 12.11).

Alternatives to Preaching

Though the spoken word often tends to predominate in church services, other forms of proclamation such as song, drama and dancing have always had a place, especially in the celebration of the greater feasts of the Church's year. Examples are the Exsultet at the Easter Vigil, mystery plays, Palm Sunday processions. The importance of visual aids such as films, banners, and the combination of all these in a 'multi-media' worship is realized more and more in these days of commercial advertising and constant television.

Furthermore, the need for the people to contribute to the proclamation in dialogue and acclamation and not just to remain passive auditors is increasingly felt. In those places where dialogue sermons and spontaneity in prayer and response have been introduced they have invariably become popular after an initial stage of hesitation due to self-consciousness and a reluctance to break through the imposed formality of traditional worship.

Response to Preaching

It is inevitable that after having listened to the word of God in the readings and the sermon people will want to vocalize their thoughts and express their praise of God and their concern for the needs of mankind in words inspired by their new understanding of the Christian message.

All that follows the sermon is in fact part of the response to preaching. It may take several forms: an appropriate hymn, the recitation of a credal formula followed by intercessions or prayers in litany form, an act of commitment, or (depending on the season or the nature of the service) of penitence and rededication, incorporating perhaps a gesture of reconciliation and peace with the community.

QUESTIONS FOR DISCUSSION

1 How ought a preacher to prepare his sermon?

2 What opportunities should be created for the discussion of the sermon and feedback?

3 To what extent are visual aids appropriate?

4 How long should a sermon last?

5 Has there been a general decline in the art of preaching or are today's sermons well adapted to today's people?

BIBLIOGRAPHY

Botte, B., *La parole dans la liturgie*. Paris 1970.

Browne, R. E. C., *The Ministry of the Word*. 2nd edn, SCM 1976.

Fuller, R. H., *What is Liturgical Preaching?* SCM 1957.

Jungmann, J. A., *The Liturgy of the Word*. Burns and Oates 1966.

Keir, T. H., *The Word in Worship*. OUP 1962.

Knox, J., *The Integrity of Preaching*. Abingdon 1957.

Milner, P., *The Ministry of the Word*. Burns and Oates 1967.

Ott, H., *Theology and Preaching*. Lutterworth 1965.

von Allmen, J. J., *Preaching and Congregation*. SCM 1962.

6

The Vocal Parts of Worship including the Content and Style of Prayers

✠

J. C. Stewart

Although the prophet Habakkuk does suggest that an appropriate response to the presence of the Lord is that all the earth should keep silence before him (Hab. 2.20 AV), and although we have it on dominical authority that we shall not be heard because of our 'much speaking' (Matt. 6.7 AV), it nevertheless seems likely that the spoken word will continue to be the main vehicle for the expression of corporate worship. The choice, arrangement, and vocal presentation of these words is therefore a matter of importance for 'words can make worship possible, or they can prevent it happening by their inadequacy or their inappropriateness.'[1]

Different Christian traditions adopt widely differing attitudes to the relative places of set forms, of free prayer and of extempore prayer.[2] In all, however, the selection and arrangement of words for worship is a matter of increasing concern. Can any criteria be established for the task?

Vocabulary

Dr J. W. Alexander's translation of Paul Gerhard's Passion hymn poses the question:

> What language shall I borrow
> To praise thee, heavenly friend?

It is a question which presses on anyone who is responsible for providing words for worship.

Bishop Ian Ramsey, in his book *Religious Language*, set out to turn the tables on logical empiricist criticism of religious language by showing how the methods of that philosophical outlook could be used to explicate the character of such language in a manner which 'can from the beginning hope to be both intellectually honest and devotionally helpful – a combination not always achieved.'[3] He characterizes the function of religious language as being to evoke a particular kind of *discernment* or *insight* which will, in turn, lead to total *commitment*. Such a conjunction of discernment and commitment is worship. One cannot, of course, guarantee that any particular words will function in this way but one of the tasks of the liturgist is surely to endeavour to arrange that it will happen as often as possible in those times and places set aside for worship. Since all the language we use of God is analogical it involves the 'borrowing' of appropriate 'models' or metaphors from other realms of discourse and the application to these models of appropriate 'qualifiers' which will indicate the 'oddness' of their use.

If we return to the hymn quoted above we may judge that friendship is an illuminating model by means of which to open up or express religious experience. Yet we know that our everyday experiences have characteristics which are not applicable here and which would make the model misleading if it were pressed too far. To give warning against that the appropriate qualifier 'heavenly' is applied as a pointer to the differences and to the depth and mystery in the situation. The danger of failing to give due attention to the need for qualifiers is amusingly (and touchingly) illustrated by Carl Burke in the postscript to his lively collection of paraphrases of scripture called *God is for Real, Man!* To the inquiry of a delinquent camper, 'What's God like, mister?' he replied confidently, 'God is like a father.' After a pause the boy replied with no little venom, 'Gee! if he was like my father I sure would hate him.'

If the symbolic character of religious language is somewhat stressed it is because the attitude described by Thomas Fawcett still prevails. He notes: 'In the age of rationalism in the eighteenth century and of materialism in the nineteenth century, it appeared to many that man had overcome the need for symbols and could know the world as it was. This attitude was often adopted not only in scientific but also in theological circles.'[4] A continuing suspicion of verbal symbolism is surely responsible for some of the flatter efforts to produce a modern language for worship.

The heart of the problem lies in those words which we use as a means of address to God or Jesus because they, as it were, establish the model from which the rest of our vocabulary flows. Ramsey points out that when the first Christians were trying to spread the gospel they used a great profusion of different models without too much concern for their coherence so long as they led to a disclosure situation. It may be that many of these now traditional models – let us take as possible examples, 'King', 'Priest', 'Redeemer', 'Righteousness' – no longer function in such a way that 'the ice breaks, the light dawns, the penny drops'. Are we inseparably wedded to them because they are biblical? Can we not be just as biblical by going into our own social milieu and practising the same kind of borrowing as was practised by the writers of Scripture?

To answer that question in the affirmative is not necessarily to be committed to throwing overboard all traditional religious vocabulary but to approach its use critically and to be freed to go beyond it. Some of the least intelligible words, like 'Amen' and 'Hallelujah', and possibly 'cherubim and seraphim' are, as Ninian Smart suggests, preserved by their very unintelligibility from reduction to the status of cliché and do significantly function as pointers to mystery, justifying their retention in forms of prayer which otherwise have gone over to a modern vernacular.[5]

Content

In considering the content of prayers we may usefully adopt the conventional analysis into the five categories of adoration, confession, petition, intercession and thanksgiving. On the whole, on formal occasions of public prayer, particularly where known set forms are not in use, it may be judged desirable to concentrate on one aspect at a time, proceeding by orderly progression from one to another rather than having them mixed indiscriminately. No particular order will be universally agreed but it may be useful for each worshipping community to have its own known order for customary use. Although there are no rules the matter is not to be decided upon on a purely arbitrary basis. It might, for instance, be thought that intercession never produces a suitable starting point and that something more positive than an extended act of confession is required at the end.

It is, perhaps, in the attempt to express *adoration* that the greatest difficulty is experienced at the present day. Here the considerations of vocabulary referred to above impinge most sharply because here the attention is most directly focused on God as he is. Much of the material that has been inherited is suggestive of the throne room of a medieval monarch or of an ancient middle-eastern potentate – models remote from the experience of modern man (even with the benefit of TV reconstructions). If the power and the love of God may be selected as two key concepts for the evoking of adoration it is important that they be held together so that we do not speak of power in a manner which is cold and impersonal (which could easily be the case if we think of that power simply in terms of the awe-inspiring immensities of the created order opened up by scientific research) nor speak of love in terms which make it anything less than awe-inspiring in its scope and depth. For this purpose we need a language which is rich and paradoxical. Where the heart is not engaged such a language may be thought to be extravagant. The danger seems unavoidable.

If many inherited or traditionally phrased prayers of adoration refer to God in terms which, for most worshippers, are no longer real and living the same may be said about the way in which many prayers of *confession* refer to man. In discussing this matter Leslie Earnshaw suggests that modern man may often have a very real sense of having lost the way, of having missed the mark, if not of positive evil; and he may have a sharper sense of corporate sin and a greater willingness to accept a 'share of responsibility for the outrage and injustice which mar the world'[6] than former generations. Yet these do not produce in him the attitude of a malefactor standing before Judge Jeffreys which many of the prayers of confession which stem directly from the Reformation seem to call for.

> O wad some Pow'r the giftie gie us
> To see oursels as others see us!
> It wad frae mony a blunder free us,
> And foolish notion.

When Robert Burns expressed his aspiration he was clearly aware of failure and folly and it is perhaps by praying that we may see ourselves in some degree as Christ sees us that we shall most readily be led to confession, whereas any attempt at castigation or catalogue will result in the mental response: 'not applicable'. Such a response merely reinforces the complacency and self-righteousness to which we are already prone. Brevity and the avoidance of a high degree of specificity may be suggested as the two most important features of a corporate prayer of confession for our times.

In *intercession* it might be argued that exactly the opposite is the appropriate prescription. Here it is the citing of specific instances and situations which are within common knowledge which brings to life the general intercessions for the church and nation, sick and suffering. There is, however, a danger in attempting to do too much in this direction on any one occasion. For instance, an endeavour to 'earth' a prayer for members of the helping professions by providing a list is as likely to offend by what it fails to mention as to help by what it includes.

Even in a modern service such as the Anglican Holy Communion Rite A – cited only because it is typical – the shape of the intercessions as a whole tends to reflect the simpler social order of a bygone day. There is no mention of any structure or groupings between the nation on the one hand and the local community and the family on the other. Yet it is by industrial and commercial enterprises, by trade unions, by the media of communication and by organized entertainment and recreation that much of the quality of life is determined.

What is believed concerning Christian character will find its expression in prayers of *petition*. The features of Christian character which are considered worthy of emphasis no doubt change from one age to another. Submissiveness, for instance, is no longer as highly thought of as it was at one time and freedom is more greatly prized. The Scripture lessons to be read on any particular occasion of worship will often suggest the particular content for the petitionary prayers on that occasion.

Many eucharistic prayers suggest that *thanksgiving* is something which ought to engage the Christians 'at all times and in all places'. Although its possible scope is unlimited – no less than the creation and salvation of the whole cosmos – yet for liturgical purposes there has to be some limitation. Particular occasions will suggest particular causes of thanksgiving and it is desirable that these should be specifically mentioned. But it is likewise desirable that these specific causes of thankfulness should be set within the context of the whole work of God; and even when neither emergent occasion nor Christian Year suggests particular points of emphasis for thanksgiving, it is important that the work of creation should not be thought of as happening only 'in the beginning' and that the work of salvation should not be thought of only in terms of distant history, but that both should be related to ongoing life as it is experienced from day to day by the worshippers.

What has been written of thanksgiving in general applies also to the eucharistic prayer of which, as the name implies, it is the chief ingredient. The eucharistic thanksgiving will specifically include the institution of the sacrament, either by reference or by recital of a narrative of institution. Different traditions and theological attitudes will indicate the desirability or otherwise of including in the eucharistic prayer such other matters as the invocation of the Holy Spirit, self-oblation and commemoration of the faithful departed.

There are other forms of prayer which do not fall easily into any of the foregoing categories. Such are the prayers of Michel Quoist which enjoy a wide popularity. Their chief use is, clearly, in private devotion. They are so highly personal and related to particular experiences that a congregation cannot relate to them as it would to other prayers. Nevertheless such material, suitably introduced, may find an occasional place in public worship as an aid to meditation.

Style

To some extent the style of a prayer will be dictated by the sort of vocabulary considered appropriate and by the content. What has been sneered at as a mere shopping-list type of prayer may, if used with appropriate pauses, be a helpful device in intercession, whereas something more carefully wrought might be considered necessary for adoration – though here, again, short bursts of acclamation might be used. Style will also be influenced by the circumstances in which or for which the prayer is produced. If a prayer is produced for a liturgy which is to be regarded as a set form, consideration will have to be given to its ability to survive frequent hearing. A turn of phrase, considered helpfully expressive or evocative in a free prayer might, after several repetitions, have become quite threadbare. Prayers to be recited corporately will require simpler sentence construction and more clear-cut rhythmical pattern than prayers which are to be spoken by a single experienced reader.

It seems improbable, however, that there are any precise rules by the careful application of which satisfactory results will be achieved. It may, however, be suggested that the sentence construction of present-day prayers ought to be such as is in general usage. The fact that Cranmer was able triumphantly to surmount the difficulties created by the un-English use of a relative clause and by other constructions derived from Latin originals is not an argument for the perpetuation of such alien features.

Nor is deliberate effort necessary to have phrase and sentence endings conform to the various forms of *cursus*. That system so widely used, especially in the Latin of the Middle Ages, is, indeed, to be found in English; but other rhythmical forms are at least as suitable for the much less polysyllabic vocabulary of English, and it has been judged that 'the sublimest effects in English are produced by the native, not the exotic, rhythm'.[7]

Dr D. L. Frost analysed the Anglican Series 3 Order for Holy Communion from the point of view of its use of rhetorical effects and concluded that its authors have achieved 'a result which would have been acclaimed in a sixteenth-century schoolroom'. He reports the result to have been achieved, however, 'without any conscious artifice' and he considers 'that the two thousand year old art of rhetoric was not more than a labelling system, masquerading as a pedagogic technique'.[8] It may therefore be concluded that it should not be allowed to dictate in the contemporary composition of prayers. What may be desirable is that the authors of public prayer, of whatever form, should have a cultivated taste which, without conscious effort, distinguishes the good from the bad and can produce that which will read and sound well, without, however, drawing attention to itself as an art form. But it is no more than desirable. Since the chief end of prayer-making is to provide a vehicle for worship, the true art, here, will be to hide itself.

Presentation

It has been assumed that we are dealing with prayers which are to be read aloud or spoken. It remains for some consideration to be given to the manner in which they and other spoken material are to be presented.

For a considerable period in the history of the Scottish Church, to take one instance, it was the practice for *everything* that was said in the course of a service to be spoken by one minister. A few verses of singing were all that was, outwardly, required of the people. Similarly in churches where a fixed form of prayers required responses of some kind to be made it is understood that the practice of leaving these entirely to another single individual was by no means unknown. It would be foolish not to recognize that a silent congregation is not necessarily a non-participating congregation. Nevertheless, there is growing agreement in most branches of the Church that some measure of vocal participation aids real participation and that the spreading of responsibility for vocal participation helps towards a better realization of the corporate nature of the Church.

The discipline of different branches of the Church may require the person speaking some of the prayers to be of an appropriate ecclesiastical status. Subject to that limitation there is little reason why, in those parts of the service where a single voice is used, that voice should always be that of a clergyman. Many congregations are, of course, quite accustomed to have lessons read by a layman and, on occasion, by children. While this practice may often be commended it should never become a matter of 'Buggins' turn'. If the scriptures are to be heard, understood and taken to heart it is necessary, first, that they should be read with sympathy and understanding. For that the person trained and set apart for their exposition may often be the best suited.

A device which can be very effective, on occasion, in reading the Bible is that suggested in the Roman Missal for the reading of the Passion narrative on Good Friday. One voice reads the narrative portions, another the words of our Lord, and a third the words of all other speakers.

Alternation of voices may also be used in certain types of prayer. An American *Experimental Liturgy Book*[9] makes much use of this device for eucharistic canons when more than one priest is present. Biddings to intercession may be spoken by one voice and summed up in a prayer spoken by another – not a new, but perhaps a somewhat under-used, practice. Where acoustics permit and smooth flow is not considered to be of pressing importance, biddings may be invited, extempore, from any member of the congregation. In some recently devised services[10] a considerable number of different voices are used in quick succession. It may be judged that in some of these the division of the prayer material is done in a somewhat arbitrary fashion and that change of voice which can, undoubtedly, help to retain attention is so frequent as to be distracting.

A more traditional practice is the antiphonal reading of psalms – leader alternating with congregation (or choir), or two parts of the congregation alternating. This might well be more widely used (*a*) where musical resources make chanting difficult or unedifying, and (*b*) where metrical versions are of such awkwardness as to render them unusable. Translations such as that of the Grail Psalter where attention has been paid to the pattern of stresses will be found of particular help. Somewhat similar in nature are the versicles and responses familiar in the services of Morning and Evening Prayer in the Book of Common Prayer. Additional sets may be devised for seasonal or occasional use and put into the hands of the congregation in duplicated form. It has been suggested that 'saying after me' in the Book of Common Prayer may originally, in places of wide-spread illiteracy, have meant exactly that – that the prayer was said phrase by phrase by the minister and repeated by the congregation. It is a device which it may still be appropriate to use where it is desired to have congregational recitation of an un-familiar prayer not in their hands.

Finally, there are texts which all will recite in unison, of which the Lord's Prayer and the historic creeds are the most familiar. Other prayers, carefully devised to aid corporate speech, may also be said together and other brief affirmations of faith may on occasion be said as response to reading or preaching when the use of the historic creeds is not required.

The writer was told by one of his parishioners, soon after she was widowed, that she had never become a communicant, nor accompanied her regularly attending husband to church because she was quite unable to sing. It was stated quite simply and sincerely as a reason, not just as an excuse. Doubtless it is a somewhat eccentric reason but it may be that it does indicate that there is need for greater opportunity for spoken participation than is often made available in many churches.

Finally, 'Let all the people say "Amen".'

NOTES

1 Leslie Earnshaw, *Worship for the Seventies*, 1973, p. 62.

2 John Huxtable, in *The Renewal of Worship*, 1965, p. 58, quotes Isaac Watts's distinction between free prayer and extemporary prayer. 'Free or "conceived" prayer is prepared before the service. It is "done by some work of meditation before we begin to speak in prayer". Extemporary prayer is spontaneous and unpremeditated – "when we without any reflection or meditation beforehand address ourselves to God and speak the thoughts of our hearts as fast as we conceive them".'

3 Ian Ramsey, *Religious Language*, 1957, 1973, p. 186.

4 Thomas Fawcett, *the Symbolic Language of Religion*.

5 Ninian Smart, *The Concept of Worship*, 1972, p. 29.

6 op. cit. p. 31.

7 A. C. Clark, *Prose Rhythms in English*.

8 R. C. D. Jasper (ed.), *The Eucharist Today*, 1974, especially pp. 151–6.

9 R. F. Hoey (ed.), *The Experimental Liturgy Book*.

10 See, for instance, the three volumes of *Celebration*, Galliard Press, 1970.

7
Music in Worship

✠

Maurice Williams

Music is an art consisting of the selection and assembly of sounds in an arranged sequence or combination. These sounds, whether produced by the human voice or by other instruments of man's devising, are non-verbal. Music is also a language, as it uses these sounds significantly. In its history, which is in all likelihood as old as humanity itself, we can trace what may be called its vocabulary, its grammar and its syntax.

The art of musical language exists in its own right, although it may also be employed in association with words, or even with some other non-verbal means of communication such as a film. It is then open to criticism; and labels like 'good' and 'bad' are attached to it. One musical work may be recognized as a creative attempt to speak the truth, and another as no more than a boring repetition of clichés. Every such judgement, however, depends on the standards or assumptions of the critic. For example, Musak is considered good by those who believe that its reproduction throughout an office block increases staff efficiency, whereas others are convinced that any such manipulative intentions are bad.

Christian worship is the celebration of the gospel. As a human activity, it also has a history. Both in structure and form the liturgy has absorbed a variety of cultural inheritances, representing the flow of the centuries and the international nature of the Church.

The interplay between these two histories of music and worship makes an intriguing study: musicians and theologians have never ceased to be in conversation with each other, although the dialogue has not always been friendly. Too fre-

46

quently, perhaps, they have been two separate groups of people, lacking an interpreter or translator who understands them both.

Two factors have complicated, and sometimes confused, the debate. The first of them is the question of the relationship between sacred and secular. In the Old Testament, for instance, while a psalmist is cheerfully declaring that 'it is a good thing . . . to sing praises' there are prophets uttering stern words about the sweet voices and seductive tunes that corrode the moral life of the people.[1] The Church Fathers similarly warned their fellows of the moral force that is inherent in music. They were particularly outspoken about the 'flute' which for them was an instrument associated with ladies of easy virtue.

But then, the secular is not of itself immoral. If it is to be distinguished from the sacred, it ought not to be separated from it. Augustine, being both a theologian and a musician, was able to apply theology not only to the use of music in church but also to the science of music itself.[2] Secular melody can be, and often has been, taken into the service of God. The famous Passion Chorale started life as a love-song, being set to the words 'My heart is distracted by a gentle maid' before it was attached to Gerhardt's 'O sacred Head'. In more recent times William Booth, Vaughan Williams and Donald Swann have each effected the transfer from secular to sacred in a distinctive way.[3]

The second of the factors is the relatively late development of music as we know it today. For the first thousand years of the Church's life, which is roughly half of Christian history to date, musical vocabulary stayed more or less settled. So the Church's practice was more or less settled too. Then polyphony appeared. And that was only the start. Between the time of that innovation and the present day the stately trot of musical evolution has lengthened its stride into a canter and then into a gallop. In consequence a multitude of new options has been opened to us. Alike through the technical developments of the art and the improving technology of instrument-making (including that most characteristic of all church instruments, the organ) the experimental possibilities have multiplied.

Such luxuriant growth has raised the question of what kind of music helps God's people to worship. The Roman Catholic

Church in this twentieth century has given the matter careful consideration. Gélineau's account of it includes a chapter entitled 'Music, Handmaid of the Liturgy'. He writes:

> As an integral, though not necessary, element in Christian worship, music, like all other arts, is dependent on the sacred action whose meaning it is intended to enrich. And when music is vocal it is dependent, in particular, on the ritual words of which it is the vehicle . . . Serving the rite humbly and nobly entails several consequences for music . . . One single principle emerges: the music of worship is functional.[4]

After the second Vatican Council, the Sacred Congregation of Rites prepared the *Instruction on Music in the Sacred Liturgy.*[5] This document sets out general norms to guide the practice of pastors, musicians and the faithful together.

In the Anglican Church the report *Music in Church* from the Archbishops' Committee appeared in 1951. It said: 'Music that is in keeping with the spirit of the liturgy will be characterized by qualities of nobility and restraint, by freedom from sensationalism or mawkishness, and from all suggestions of secularity.' Since then, bodies such as the RSCM have produced further reports giving valuable guidance.

The Church of Scotland's *Handbook to the Church Hymnary* (1979) observes:

> The church musician may sound a little self-righteous . . . if he replies that he is not simply a religious entertainer paid to give people what they want. Like the preacher, he must always try to be *intelligible* but he need not always try to be *popular* . . . Weak, effeminate, sentimental music can as effectively distort our image of God in Christ as can weak, effeminate, sentimental pictures – or words.

Such advice may sound at first to be unduly restrictive. If we ask within what framework such judgements are made about the practice of the musical art before God, we meet once again the interplay of two histories. Our concern is with music in worship. The first consideration, therefore, is to hold fast to that which is good. Here, to start with, the musician is master. From within his own discipline he will help us to recognize the marks of craftsmanship or the lack of it. But that must not be the end of the matter.

> There is no way in this world by which we can arrive at the conclusion that Bach is better than Brahms ... As it happens, Bach knew what the Church was about, and Brahms did not, which makes Bach a better church musician than Brahms; but not a better musician. And yet we do say that Bach is better than Stainer ...[6]

So the second consideration is to express what the Church is about. And here the theologian becomes our conductor. From within his discipline, he declares that everything which happens in the liturgical celebration serves God, being directed to him. Music which serves God adorns worship, and so it serves the gospel. As a vehicle of the Church's worship, music has no autonomy but only a ministerial function. Take, for instance, any hymn tune. The words of that hymn should themselves be 'good', both in craftsmanship and content, which is to say that they should be witness to Christ – incarnate, crucified and risen. Then, as text, they are the agenda for the church musician. His work, when it is composed and played and sung, must not contradict them. The music's language, in its own idiom, shares the calling of its text to bear witness to the gospel. Otherwise we should have what R. E. C. Browne pointed to as a possibility in ill-prepared preaching – the holding of two contradictory doctrines at the same time, albeit one of them unconsciously.

Most church music is written to accompany some liturgical text. There is, however, a place within the worship of God's people for incidental music without words. It is ruled by the same canon: it adorns worship because it serves God. Its ministerial function is that of *enabling* the congregation to worship.

> We have to distinguish between all musical utterances used to dispose men to worship, in the way that architecture and applied fine art can dispose men to worship, and all musical utterances used as the immediate vehicle of the spirit of worship itself ... We must, for good, open the gates to the two orders of church music.[7]

And there the theologian rests his case. He has nothing to say about music whose origins lie in the secular world, nor about the relative virtues of the musical idiom that derives from any particular period of history. In all such matters he continues his friendly conversation with the musician. For the theologian has a ministerial function too. He can, and must, put up a 'Road Closed' sign at those avenues which, however legitimate a thoroughfare they may be in the concert-hall, are not entered in the liturgy.[8] He can, and must, then listen to the artist.

The third consideration is performance. Let us now assume we have some good music written for worship. It matters not whether it be for organ or orchestra to play, or for a congregation or choir to sing. It is at this moment only a score, printed symbols on paper. So it is not yet truly music. It becomes that as it is performed. In this it bears a certain resemblance to Holy Scripture. While the book is shut, it is not the word. It requires reading. But some lectors are better than others, as some practical musicians are better than others. Here also the Church must strive for the good while accepting the less than good, if that is the best of which it is capable. For whereas the majority of worshippers will never be called on to read Scripture in the liturgical assembly, all of them will have some part in the performance of the music. At no point is it more important to remember that the direction of Christian worship is to *God*. He it is who, though not countenancing the slipshod, receives our all too imperfect offering in his grace.

NOTES

1 Ps. 92.1; Amos 5.23–4; Isa. 5.11–12.

2 Augustine, *De Musica.*

3 Lecture by Sir Thomas Armstrong, printed in *The Journal of the Baptist Music Society*, vol. 3, no. 2.

4 J. Gélineau, *Voices and Instruments in Christian Worship*, 1964, p. 46.

5 Published in English translation by the Catholic Truth Society.

6 E. Routley, *Music Sacred and Profane*, p. 183.

7 Walford Davies and Harvey Grace, *Music and Worship*, 1935, pp. 18–20.

8 cf. Karl Barth, C.D. IV.3.ii, p. 866: the congregation is 'not a choral society. Its singing is not a concert.'

8

Silence in Worship

✠

Ronald Jasper

There is evidence that the Christian Church recognized silence as an integral part of the liturgy at an early date. Canon 19 of the Council of Laodicea (*c.* 345 AD) enjoined silence with the first of the three Prayers of the Faithful, while a few years later the Apostolic Constitutions made provision for it at the Offertory. A century later the Homilies of Narsai go much further, stating that silence should be observed from the Sursum Corda to the Sanctus, and during the Canon until after the Institution Narrative. Furthermore, a number of early writers – notably St John Chrysostom and St Cyril of Jerusalem – stressed the attitude of awe which should surround the sacrament, implying the element of silence. It is well expressed in the famous hymn from the Liturgy of St James:

> Let all mortal flesh keep silence,
> and with fear and trembling stand;
> ponder nothing earthly-minded,
> for with blessing in his hand,
> Christ our God to earth descendeth,
> our full homage to demand.

At an early date, both in East and West, silence in the liturgy would appear to have been achieved, not only by the congregation remaining silent, but also by the recitation of certain prayers – particularly during the Canon – in a subdued or inaudible voice by the celebrant. This was described as 'mystic', expressing on the part of the priest and designed to evoke in the laity an attitude of awe and reverence in the presence of God.

In the sixth century the Emperor Justinian objected to the silent recitation of the Canon – a practice which was then fairly widespread if not universal. He tried to suppress it by legislation in 565, but his efforts appear to have had no permanent effect. By the eighth century the 'mystical' recitation of the Canon was an established fact in the East, while Ordo Romanus II testifies that a similar practice was current in the West by the same date.

Opinions may differ as to the desirability of the silent or 'mystical' recitation of certain prayers in a liturgy: nevertheless both the spread and the persistence of the practice bear witness to a devotional need for silence in public worship. In the West, for example, the growth and popularity of Low Masses in the Middle Ages owed something to this instinctive appreciation of the value of silence, with the opportunities it offered for private prayer. It is also evident in the Church of England today, where many worshippers still prefer a said 'quiet' Communion service early in the morning to a choral Eucharist at a later hour with a far greater number of people.

The Reformers of the sixteenth century, however, saw little merit in the silent 'mystical' recitation of prayers; and this element disappeared from the worship of the Reformed Churches. A comment by Martin Bucer expresses the situation clearly:

The purpose of all the Church's observances is the effective building up of faith in Christ. This requires that whatever is said and done in the sacred assemblies is fully understood by everyone present (1 Cor. 14); that whatever is taught from the holy scripture is received as the teaching of God; and whatever is said in the prayers and thanksgivings is said from the faith and the heart of everyone present as in the sight of God. Clearly therefore it is a matter of absolute necessity that the ministers of churches should recite these prayers and psalms and lessons with the greatest solemnity and devotion; in a clear and expressive voice; and from a point from which everything they say can be easily heard by everyone present. By these means faith will effectively be renewed. A place must therefore be appointed for the recitation of these sacred things, and solemnity and clarity required of ministers in reciting them; and this must be achieved not only by barren exhortation and written instructions but in such a way that a strict and vigilant performance follows upon the command.[1]

But it was not only the silent recitation of prayers which disappeared: silence itself had little place in Reformed worship. Some years ago Professor W. D. Maxwell deplored this 'neglect of silence', and suggested that it may have been partly a result of the method of conducting worship in the Reformed Churches:

> a method that relies almost entirely upon the spoken word for direction, and not at all upon ceremonial . . . In worship directed largely by ceremonial – that is by action rather than speech – opportunity for directed silent prayer constantly recurs; but worship that demands upon the spoken voice for leadership and direction is almost inevitably defective in this respect.[2]

But even in the Book of Common Prayer, with its ample provision of rubrics, provision for silence is made only on an isolated occasion, namely, in the Ordinal where, after the examination of the candidates for ordination to the priesthood, the congregation is asked to pray for them – 'for the which Prayers there shall be silence kept for a space'. Apparently no such provision was considered necessary in the case of deacons and bishops. Silence played no part in public Reformed worship, and its absence was exemplified in the description of Anglican Morning and Evening Prayer as 'a brisk verbal trot with singularly little breathing space'.

One community for whom silence meant a great deal, however, was the Society of Friends. For them it has been a basic ingredient of their worship; and Professor Horton Davies has suggested that it is due to their influence that the Reformed Churches have increasingly come to recognize its value.[3] In current Anglican and Reformed forms of service growing provision is made for silence, notably in connection with the reading of Scripture, penitence, intercessions and thanksgivings. The same is true of the new Roman rites, with the additional significant provision that there is no longer to be a silent recitation of the eucharistic prayers. It should be remembered, however, that for the Quakers silence meant something quite different from the mere absence of noise. 'It is a Living Silence, as the Quakers named it long ago, and it is no negative thing; it is rather a deliberate and joyous withdrawal from the world of sense and time into that deeper part of our being which belongs to eternity.'[4]

Otto has analysed what we might call 'Quaker Silence' and sees in it three elements.[5] Primarily the Quakers observed silence for waiting: this was a detachment from various outward distractions and an inward concentration, by means of which the worshipper prepared for the coming of God and his message. This then passed over into the silence of sacrament – the *numen praesens*: the insufficient became event: God was in the midst. Finally from this came the achievement of unity, the silence of fellowship and communion. It is silence such as this that we should attempt to realize in our worship today. In a world which is increasingly full of noise and bustle, we should take care that our worship is likewise not beset by noise and bustle. Rather it should contain an element of restful waiting upon God, which opens the 'subconscious' or 'unconscious' mind to the influence of divine grace. Periods of silence in the liturgy should therefore not be mere meaningless pauses when nothing at all happens for the congregation, because the minister is either busy saying his own private prayers, or because he is saying inaudibly public prayers which he should be saying aloud. Rather these periods of silence are 'directed' to some particular purpose or end. In such silences men may pray individually and independently, yet the action is a corporate action. Indeed it would be true to say that no other form of public prayer combines individual and corporate expression so perfectly.

Certain elements in public worship lend themselves naturally to silence. It can be a valuable element in intercession and thanksgiving, particularly when preceded by biddings, and concluded by a collect, or a versicle and response, or some prayer such as the General Thanksgiving, or the Lord's Prayer said corporately. Similarly a period of silence for self-examination is eminently desirable before a congregation says together a general confession. Silence can be equally 'directed', but be of a more meditative kind after the reading of lessons, the preaching of a sermon, or the singing of a hymn, or even the playing of a piece of music. Or again, there can be directed silence before or after or during the reception of the sacraments. In the Church of Scotland, the reception of communion in complete silence is a significant example.

But silence, like other things of value, cannot be found easily. For those who are not used to it, two minutes of silence can appear an incredibly long time, as it does for many people on Remembrance Day. It requires a discipline of mind and body. In public worship, therefore, periods of silence should be fairly brief and guidance should be given as to their use. Care, experience and sensitivity are necessary in deciding both duration and frequency, and these may well vary from day to day according to circumstances.

Finally, some readers may find it useful to consider silence in the context of a description of worship written by the late Archbishop William Temple:

> To worship is to quicken the conscience by the holiness of God, to feed the mind with the truth of God, to purge the imagination by the beauty of God, to open the heart to the love of God, to devote the will to the purpose of God. All this is gathered up in that emotion which cleanses us from selfishness because it is the most selfless of all emotions – adoration.[6]

NOTES

1 E. C. Whitaker, *Martin Bucer and the Book of Common Prayer,* 1974, p. 14.
2 W. D. Maxwell, *Concerning Worship*, 1948, p. 70.
3 Horton Davies, *Worship and Theology in England, 1690–1850*, 1961, p. 11.
4 Geoffrey Hoyland, *The Use of Silence*, pp. 11–12.
5 R. Otto, *The Idea of the Holy*, tr. J. W. Harvey, 1924, pp. 216–20.
6 W. Temple, *The Hope of a New World*, p. 30.

9
Movement and Drama in Worship

A. Stewart Todd

While an impressive amount of agreement is achieved in our day on the essentials of worship there can be no doubt that there remains, among churches and within churches, controversy on the matters comprehended in the title of this chapter.

There are many who will question whether the dramatic element and the element of movement have any real place in worship and will contend that such movement and drama as there are should be reduced to the barest minimum. Certainly one remembers churches where great architectural ingenuity has been expended on achieving this very simplicity, where a vestry has been built on a mezzanine floor so that it could give a clergyman direct access to the pulpit, a door doubling as the vestry door and sounding board of the pulpit. The clergyman, having appeared there with admirable unobtrusiveness, remains there on all but perhaps two Sundays in the year when he descends to celebrate at the Table. Even for baptism, certainly in the past and perhaps still in a few places, he would lean over the pulpit to administer the sacrament, water being provided in a bowl held by a bracket fixed to the pulpit. The movement of the people likewise is often reduced to the minimum, entry and exit being by short aisles connecting with a series of doors. Apart from rising and sitting down for praise and prayer there may be no other movement during the entire service, offerings having been collected in a vestibule at the beginning and having gone directly to the count. When Holy Communion is celebrated the same economy of movement is practised. The point is that it is still considered a merit, whether or not its merit is understood by all; it is considered a feature of the Reformed tradition; it is safe-

56

guarded by a liturgical fundamentalism and will not lightly be abandoned. The Scriptures say, after all, 'Be still, and know that I am God'. (Ps. 46.10 AV).

Ironically our Eastern Orthodox friends, who are certainly not afraid of movement and drama in worship, would argue that stillness is the one thing lacking in worship such as has been described above; that the congregational movements that are its main characteristic create an effect not so much of simplicity as of restlessness, and the disciplined nature of those movements militates against that spiritual freedom in which men and women do come to know that God is God.

Given then that we are dealing with a controversial subject and that in the constituency where we seek to arouse interest there are those for whom movement to a prayer desk or to a lectern is high liturgical adventure, it seems important that arguments put forward concerning movement and drama should be theologically well founded so that they are not dismissed as the extravagances of an over-developed aesthetic apperception.

There are elements in worship which are quite basic and for which dominical authorization can be claimed. Let us consider only those elements for the moment. The word of God must be preached: the Eucharist must be celebrated: the people of God must come together to do these things.[1] The word is to be preached to all nations and when they are baptized they are to be taught all that the Lord has commanded (Matt. 28.20). The Eucharist is likewise divinely commanded. Gathering together in Jesus' name is implicitly if not explicitly commanded in Matt. 18.20 (cf. 1 Cor. 1.2). We may identify these as the Lord's minimal requirements for worship: we may go farther and assert that because these are the requirements of the Lord of the Church they contain within themselves an implicit negative, namely, that nothing should be allowed in worship which is not subservient to these basic requirements. The area between these outer limits is considerable, however, and this is the area of freedom, the freedom granted to the Church which has heard the word of God through the Holy Spirit. It is an eschatological freedom: it is freedom to serve the Lord of the Church. It is freedom to use any of the forms and fashions of the world in this service of the Lord. It is something quite different from human predilection or whim. It is, however, a considerable area of freedom, in which

C

we are free to sing metrical psalms or prose psalms, to have fermented wine or unfermented wine, to have read prayers or extempore prayers, symbols, gestures, clergy in gorgeous vestments or sombre black Genevan gowns, to encourage movement or to desist from movement, in which above all we are free to learn from one another. This is the area in which liturgy develops and has a history, where in the freedom of the Spirit the Church takes from the world, from its language and its art and music, new forms and presses them into the service of word and sacrament. Everything that is done must be done in a way that is appropriate to the mighty mystery that worship is, and to the interpenetration of the human and divine that characterizes it. What is done must be appropriate to the overruling presence of the Lord in worship: it must be appropriate to the capacity and to the circumstances of his people. That capacity and these circumstances will change from time to time and from age to age, and therefore what is done or not done in the area of freedom will change – ought to change. The Spirit we have received is not a spirit of slavery . . . but a Spirit that makes us sons and we should not fear (Rom. 8.15). We are therefore free to move and to be moved in worship.

It is now important to add one more word of basic definition of worship and that is to state that it is an action. We have said above that it is characterized by an interpenetration of the human and the divine: perhaps that ought to read interaction: perhaps it ought to be still further refined to stress that the primary action is the action of God and the action of the worshipper is reaction. The important thing is that it is action. Karl Barth calls it 'the most momentous, the most urgent, the most glorious action that can take place in human life'.

Of course it is arbitrary to say the action of worship starts at this point or at that point: and of course circumstances are different in different parishes and the geography of church buildings differs enormously from one to another, but if what is said in the quotation above is true, then one must ask whether a casual forgathering and a disorderly drifting into the worship area is wholly appropriate. For good sociological reasons the right thing for worshippers to do in some parishes may be to gather before the hour of worship and have a chat with one another over breakfast or coffee, but for equally good theological reasons they might very well thereafter enter the worship area in procession:

> ye are come unto mount Sion and unto the city of the living God, the heavenly Jerusalem, and to an innumerable company of angels, to the general assembly and church of the firstborn, which are written in heaven, and to God the Judge of all, and to the spirits of just men made perfect, and to Jesus . . . (Heb. 12.22–4).

Similarly if all the things we say about the Eucharist are right, if we have truly been 'satisfied with the food of the faithful, the bread of heaven and the wine that maketh most glad the heart of man' and if there is now the possibility for us of walking a bit more faithfully in the steps of our Lord then again it seems probable that some minimal choreography might represent that transition. If nothing can be devised to be put in place of a haphazard congregational dispersal then at least clergy and those assisting in any distinctive way in the service could surely move away in some ordered manner on behalf of the congregation. But this is only the beginning. Perhaps we have something to learn about movement from the Orthodox, from their Little Entry and Great Entry. Then there will be Sundays in the year when the procession will take on a special character – obvious Sundays like Palm Sunday and Harvest Festival, but there are others like Mothering Sunday or Plough Sunday where the movement will point beyond itself to some basic truth at the heart of that day's celebration and the procession will therefore be appropriate and in the full sense of the word edifying. It may also be reasonable to suggest that the skill of the artist might be employed to better purpose in providing symbols to be carried in these processions than in adorning pieces of church furniture with them – pieces which are often in themselves sufficient symbols, the simplicity and directness of which should not be overlaid.

Not only beginnings and endings but all the movements of the liturgy need constantly to be reviewed to see if they are appropriate to the action in hand and if they make imaginative use of the freedom in Christ which the Church enjoys. We become aware therefore of the whole subject of ceremonial not as an optional extra but as an integral part of the rite. The Offertory is a moment in the service which has received much imaginative attention in recent times. Not all of this has been wise and there have been times when the limitations on our freedom have not been observed and the lordship of Christ has been momentarily forgotten and, dramatically speaking, the sacrifice of Christ has been overshadowed by our sacrifices with all their Pelagian overtones.[2]

Clearly the detail of eucharistic ceremonial varies greatly in different Churches. A gesture of elevation or of fraction deserves thought but not so much thought that it constitutes a climactic moment where such a moment is unwarranted. In this area willingness to learn from observation of one another is one of the prime requisites.

The dispensing of the elements is however an action which deserves the most careful study by Churches and fear of innovation and experiment must be conquered. Clearly there is merit in a mode of distribution that represents community rather than individualism. Clearly there is merit in moving out of pews towards a table: there is merit to standing in a circle around a table or to sitting at a table. On the debit side this may involve an unwelcome degree of noise and commotion. There can be a quiet orderliness in bringing elements to the pews. There can be no definitive arrangement but there ought to be experiment and an honest seeking after the happiest solution. Whatever solution is found it seems important to stress that the scale of movement and action involved should be carefully related to the whole Eucharist. We are commanded not only to share bread and wine but to give thanks and bless. The emotional centre of gravity is in the eucharistia, the grateful, confessional anamnesis of the Great Prayer. This buoyancy of faith is lost if the ensuing distribution of elements takes too long. It may also be lost if clasping our Christian brother or sister to our hearts is so elaborate and lengthy a process that it outweighs our endeavour to clasp Christ to ourselves in close-companioned, inarticulate silence and through him to have communion with God.

We turn now to think of more adventurous movement in the liturgy and first to think of the possible contribution drama might make in helping to expound the word of God and the response of the worshipper to it. A scientist[3] was recently quoted as saying that the eye is the key to increased perception and that methods should be devised to make more use of the great capacity of the human eye for absorbing information. He spoke of the lesser capacities of the human ear, which required a slow sequential method in which one word followed another. A map was an example of how a great deal of information could be passed to the brain in a much shorter time, by the use of the eye. Clearly this has implications for the liturgy. The time available in modern worship for communication of biblical truth, for example, is much shorter than in the past and for many people occasional participation in the liturgy may be the only education to which they are exposed. It has to be asked whether we can afford to cling to our word-dominated liturgies. Also if it is true that children belong at the Eucharist with their parents, and if, as is possible, their Christian education cannot be guaranteed at day-school, then perhaps some biblical truth must be communicated to them as well as to adults. The slow sequential method in which one word follows another then becomes slower and clumsier and truth addressed to the eye has much to commend it.

Modern exegesis of the Book of Psalms has uncovered one after another reference to action and drama in Temple worship or to symbolism powerfully acted out, especially on festival occasions. The ceremonial for the day of Atonement where Aaron (Lev. 16), laying his hands on the goat and confessing the sins of Israel over it, symbolically transfers the sins to the animal and then drives it into the wilderness must have been immensely dramatic.

Drama, sometimes bizarre, is found in the prophets. In Ezekiel, for example, the word of God is communicated powerfully and poignantly in high drama – messages of great urgency and seriousness. Jesus' frequent use of visual aids reveals his awareness of the value of engaging the eye. He does not invite his hearers merely to think about a coin, he has one in his hand; he does not merely ask them to think about a child, he brings one into the circle of his hearers. For drama one thinks of the feeding of the five thousand or any of the miracles. They were after all dramatic enactments of eschatological truth. One thinks above all of the cleansing of the Temple where in high drama the symbolism of the Court of the Gentiles is reinstated and Jesus reaffirms the old religious ideal of the mission of the Jews to the whole world. If there is little evidence of dramatic presentation

61

in the Christian Church before the fourth century, that may simply be because the celebration of the Eucharist began in private houses which did not lend themselves to drama. The missionary value of dramatic representations of biblical truth was however recognized in the Middle Ages in the production of miracle and morality plays. Clearly this art-form has much to offer and a drama group might well be as important an instrument in worship as a choir.[4]

What about dance? The monopoly of the organ has at last been challenged: even the guitar has been exorcized of its twentieth-century demon-possession and baptized into the liturgy. What hinders the dance from being baptized? The Old Testament precedents are familiar. Miriam danced (Exod. 15.20–21). David 'danced before the Lord with all his might'. We are summoned in the psalms to praise God's name with the dance (Ps. 149.3 AV), with the timbrel and dance (Ps. 150.4 AV). In an extra-liturgical performance of, say, Vaughan Williams' *Mass in G Minor* it is scarcely conceivable that in the Sanctus, for example, the conductor should be simply a metronome and should not respond to the music with some eloquent movement of his arms and indeed his whole body. But if that movement seems so integral a part of the performance outside the liturgy why should it not be serviceable within the liturgy and thereafter why should that movement not be developed by a separate group of people as dance? It is after all with angels and archangels and all the company of heaven that we share the Sanctus. Botticelli's angels sing at the Nativity: they also dance with a beautiful rhythm of limbs and draperies that conveys joy to us irresistibly, passionately. There are few who would question the validity of Botticelli's vision. Mortals can move joyously and passionately. There is at least a case for a dance group in a church as well as a drama group and choir.

There are some however who make the point that all the worshippers should be moved physically in the same way as they may all be moved emotionally. J. G. Davies argues cogently not only that dance, congregational dance, is appropriate to worship but that it is so appropriate that the Church ought to resume its old role of patron of the arts and positively encourage it in the liturgy.[5] The idea that we can convert a congregation from its alternation of frozen immobility and disciplined movements of standing and sitting to free, unselfconscious, uninhibited, joyous, communal dance sounds ludicrous: it is not wrong. We are free to do it and Davies is right in many of his insights about the nature of dance – a non-discursive language, an art-form that underlines the unity of soul and body, an activity that involves the participants self-sacrificially with one another. If what Barth says in the sentence quoted earlier is true, then of course dancing as an art-form is as appropriate as it ever was in the Book of Psalms and we must listen attentively to the testimony of those who have experienced congregational dance in this country.[6] On the other hand while dance may be appropriate to the divine in worship it must be seriously questioned whether it is appropriate to the human – in other words whether it is suited to the capacity and the circumstances of many congregations at this time. As Davies acknowedges, the present century has seen the virtual demise of communal dancing.[7] Indeed the dance at the moment is embarrassingly divisive. There are dances for the young and dances for the old and, in Scotland at least, country dancing has additional social overtones. A whole new process of re-education would appear to be necessary and one would guess it would come fairly low on most congregations' list of educational priorities. For those communities for whom dance is a natural form of play (and Christians are of all people most entitled to play because of salvation), there is good reason for giving it a place in the liturgy.

The Church must take all proper precautions in employing the arts in the liturgy, recognizing the limitations of art-forms which unless they are carefully disciplined are a 'speaking with tongues' that is less useful than 'prophecy'; nevertheless she ought, in the freedom granted to her, to be imaginative, inventive and careful not to neglect any art-form which brings eloquence to the words and actions of worship – that great and glorious mystery which stands at the very heart of her life and service.

NOTES

1 cf. Peter Brunner, *Zur Lehre vom Gottesdienst: Leiturgia IV*, pp. 272ff.
2 cf. *Studia Liturgica*, vol. 3, no. 4, pp. 228ff.

3 Sir Hermann Bondi, FRS, Chief Scientist at the Department of Energy, giving the opening lecture at the International Congress of Aerospace Medicine, quoted in *The Times*, 5 September 1978.

4 Anne Long, *Praise Him in the Dance*.

5 J. G. Davies, *New Perspectives on Worship Today*, 1978, pp. 16–40.

6 cf. David Watson, *I Believe in the Church*, 1978, pp. 195ff.

7 op. cit., p. 35.

10
Posture and Worship

— ✠ —

Donald McIlhagga

The giving to our whole lives the character of worship is one of the revolutions of the gospel. From the point of view of an incarnational faith life and liturgy, worship and the world, are not to be seen in isolated compartments. If we believe Christianity is about God's relation to the whole *person*, and if we believe the body is the temple of the Spirit of God (1 Cor. 3.16), then what our bodies do in worship is important. If we believe we should offer our whole selves to God as our 'spiritual worship' (Rom. 12.1–2), then in addition to the way we focus our minds and our wills, the way we *feel* with our bodies in worship is important.

We know that as individuals we are 'one', we are a 'unity'. We are familiar with 'psychosomatic' theories explaining how the mind can affect the body. We are becoming familiar with the reverse side of that coin – the ways in which the body can reveal what we really think, despite what we may *want* others to think; how the body can reveal what we really feel regardless of what we want others to think we feel. If we do not want to relate closely to someone, then despite conversation our eyes will not meet their eyes. If we are ashamed then, without consciously deciding to do so, we will hang our head. So not only should we expect our beliefs and our attitudes to affect the 'body language'[1] of our worship, we should be prepared to ask what in fact the 'body language' of our worship says about our attitudes and our beliefs. Is not this an area in which we should quite literally be able to feel the link between God and our daily experience?

In this respect what applies to individuals will also apply to a community. The 'body language' of the Church will speak as loudly as the words we use in worship of what the Church really believes and really has to say. Are there points in the liturgy where the congregation stands, where it kneels? Or does it sit for most of the time? Are there times when there is movement, or when there is stillness? What are such times really saying? If a visitor walks in to Sunday worship will what we are doing help him to say 'Yes' to the gospel? (cf. 1 Cor. 14.16).

There will be some who look for uniformity and decry the present state of affairs in worship as confusion. You can go to one church and folk will be kneeling at a rail to receive the bread and wine of the Eucharist. You can go to the next and folk will remain seated in their fixed pews. At another they will stand round an altar table and share the loaf and cup hand to hand. Sometimes a variety of experience can be found in one church.

If there is unconsidered following of a tradition 'handed down', then 'confusion' may indeed be the right word, but if the action is thought through by the local congregation and done as that which is 'right' and 'appropriate' to that local situation, then it is no longer confusion but an example of the variety and diversity that enriches our unity in Christ. If a greater degree of variety within one local fellowship is desired, then the *setting* for worship will have to be considered carefully, and in particular whether our church furnishings inhibit the postures we think we should adopt. This may be particularly true of the manner in which we administer the Eucharist. Can a balance between good order and flexibility be achieved?

At the centre of our worship what we do with the symbols of bread and wine will reveal much about the nature of the faith. If we use one loaf and a common cup then we demonstrate the corporate nature of the Church (1 Cor. 10.16). If we use wafers or separate wine glasses we are in danger of veering towards the heresy of individualism. This danger is present in a method of administering the bread and wine when one officiant serves each individual in turn. If, however, we share the elements from hand to hand, whether seated in the pews or preferably standing round the altar table, we are not only emphasizing the corporate nature of the action but are learning that as we are served by our neighbour so the Lord serves us, and as we serve our neighbour so we can be Christ to him. The corporate nature of the action will be emphasized if, when a group is at the altar table, communicants wait until the group is dismissed, possibly with a word of Scripture. If the distribution of the symbols is from the altar table president to the servers and then to the people, we are reminded that Christ himself is the host at the sacrament and that his grace must spread through his people to the world. This would be a method of serving the sacrament which gives us an important example of how we use our bodies in worship. Is this not a way which makes the people active participants rather than merely passive receivers, and therefore highly desirable?

Corporateness is primary in worship; so a uniformity of posture might be expected in the other major parts of a liturgy. The posture would then be part of the total presentation of the drama of an act of worship. Clear instructions enable people to know what their part is, not as 'audience' but as participants in the drama.

Some practices are almost universal, such as standing to sing, though there is a good case for using a more appropriate posture if there be one for a particular hymn or psalm being sung. There are some practices which are general within a particular denomination or tradition. Anglicans will almost invariably kneel for the blessing at the end of worship, but if this action is to be seen also as a dismissal, as a sending out into the world, then sometimes it would be appropriate for it to be received standing and be followed immediately by departure into the world.

Liturgy should be flexible enough within the locally accepted tradition to add meaning by varying certain postures from time to time, though careful thought should be given to the way to initiate any change. We may ask whether there are any guidelines for the postures we might generally use in worship, for example, in prayer? Should we simply accept traditional postures? If we belong to a tradition in which the posture is the same for all prayer, probably sitting or kneeling, then it may indeed be an advance in real worship to accept, say, the possibility of standing. In general within the Church in recent years kneeling has become associated with penitence and standing with thanksgiving. But we come to worship to focus our normal everyday lives and we might ask whether what we do really relates to the natural human postures of life. Perhaps the most natural sign of penitence is the hanging of the head which can be done more easily standing or sitting than kneeling. The bending of the knee is more clearly associated in life with begging someone to do something, therefore with supplication and intercession.

Perhaps the most natural bodily expression of thanks is the embrace. Would this best be symbolized in worship by holding hands in a circle? Such an action would have added meaning if the thankgiving were the central eucharistic prayer literally gathered round the altar table. Again congregations will vary, but decisions must be made – and it is to be hoped not by default – on the most appropriate postures to adopt for the main elements of worship, for the beginning, for singing, listening, reading, for penitence, supplication and intercession, for affirmation, thanksgiving and sharing, and for the ending.

Within the corporate action of worship, individuals can often feel free to 'do their own thing' and actions expressing individual response to God can be accepted without embarrassment. If the communion elements are served to people in their places, then they should feel free to sit or kneel. If all are standing for thanksgiving and individuals can best express their praise by raising their hands high in the air, then this should be possible without others feeling 'put off'. Is the guideline for an individual 'be yourself' within the discipline of the corporateness of the action? We must not be insensitive to the other people present. It is possible to err on the side of 'enthusiasm' and an unnecessary maximizing of body posture. In an act of supplication to insist on enough space to be prostrate might be unreasonable. In the 'kiss of peace' to give a 'bear-hug' to a total stranger might be inappropriate. But equally we may err on the side of reticence and an unnatural minimizing of body posture. In an act of penitence if an individual feels so inhibited as to deny himself the opportunity of, say, kneeling or making the sign of the cross as part of the acceptance of forgiveness, or if in the 'kiss of peace' a husband and wife can only bring themselves formally to shake hands, then people are being denied a full offering of themselves in worship. The wisdom of the 1549 Prayer Book is unlikely to be bettered: 'as touching, kneeling, crossing, holding up of hands, knocking upon the breast and other gestures, they may be used or left, as every man's devotion serveth without blame'.

The subject of posture in worship is part of the larger topic of the body in worship and the part played by our senses and indeed our sexuality.[2] A fuller consideration would in particular have considered how the sense of touch relates to worship postures. In all this, what we do together as a Christian community must have prior consideration, but of increasing importance in our day is also the freedom which we as individuals must feel to offer our whole beings to God in response to his offer of himself to us. Just as no two people are the same, so no two sets of local circumstances are the same, and different conclusions will be arrived at in different places on this whole question. The important thing is that these conclusions should be determined by the group which gathers together.

NOTES

1 See Desmond Morris, *Manwatching*.
2 J. G. Davies, *New Perspectives on Worship Today*, 1978, p. 3.

11
Family Services

✠

A. Raymond George

In 1975 the Joint Liturgical Group published *Worship and the Child* (ed. R. C. D. Jasper). In this there were chapters from various denominational standpoints on children at worship, and the term 'Family Service' frequently occurred, with accounts of how such services work, how they are regarded in various styles of churchmanship, and what problems they raise. But the varying views of the term and the growing demand for material for use in such services lead us to go into the matter again.

The term 'Family Service' is indeed hard to define; for it is used in different denominations in different ways. The principal service of the Christian family, the local church, is the Eucharist, but there is some danger if its exclusive aspect is always ignored and its solemnity lost in the atmosphere of celebration and warm welcome, or indeed if its mysteries are for ever being adapted to the uninitiated. Accordingly varying types of services are devised which particularly emphasize that Christian worship is for the whole family of God, which includes children as well as their parents and other adults. Children, it is often rightly said, are not 'the Church of the future'; they are part of the Church of the present, and they must be treated as persons in their own right with their own gifts to bring and need of help. But the problems of the adult world must not be imposed upon them too soon, which is why they should not always be present for the whole of the Church's proclamation and prayer. Hence comes the use of the term 'Family Services', which may serve to emphasize that all services are for the entire family, but more usually contrasts such services with other types of service at which children are not encouraged to be present.

We have said that the principal service is the Eucharist, and this represents the ideal, but in practice in some traditions the Sunday morning service is a word-service which only monthly or quarterly leads into the Lord's Supper, in some the best-attended service is the Morning Prayer and sermon, the Eucharist being held at some time such as 8 a.m.; in some there are several Eucharists, one of which may be more prominent than others. Therefore in what follows we use the term 'principal service' to indicate that Sunday morning service which is attended by the largest congregation and is viewed as their main normal central act of worship.

There are at least four ways of viewing Family Services, which are sometimes called 'Family Church Services' to emphasize that the whole Church has the making of a family.

(1)   *One Mass is a Children's Mass.* In the Roman Catholic tradition, there is such emphasis on the Mass that, though sometimes services of the word are held for children, the service at which children are expected to be present on Sundays is usually the Mass, and out of a whole series of Masses on a Sunday one may be designated 'Children's Mass' and be simpler in style than the others. The Roman Catholic Church has provided a *Directory on Children's Masses* and special eucharistic prayers for Masses with children. Their use 'is restricted to Masses which are celebrated with children only or Masses at which the majority of the participants are children.'

'A community of children' is 'one consisting of children who have not yet reached the age of preadolescence'.

Such Masses are of course used in the schools on weekdays, but may also be used on Sundays. They are not fully 'Family Services' because the whole emphasis is on children almost to the exclusion of adults; but they bear some resemblance to the Family Services of other communions. In Anglican churches there is no official provision of texts for children's Eucharists, but sometimes a children's Eucharist is held, celebrated in a simple way, perhaps with spoken explanations.

(2)   *Children are present for a time at the principal service.* In the Church of Scotland and the Free Churches there is usually only one service on Sunday mornings and one on

71

Sunday evenings. The view is often taken that the Sunday morning service (unlike the Sunday evening service) is for adults and children alike, and accordingly it is described as 'Family Worship', and sometimes children are present throughout it. But since the decline in afternoon Sunday schools, it is often combined with morning Sunday school or 'Junior Church'. The children usually withdraw to their own lessons after ten or fifteen minutes; but while they are present some regard is paid to their presence, as, for example, by the choice of the second hymn. Sometimes a brief 'children's address' is given, though in some places this custom is dying out. Another method is that, instead of going out after the beginning, they come in before the end. Similarly Anglican churches may incorporate various arrangements for children in the principal service, sometimes in that case called 'Family Eucharist'. Such an arrangement is hardly possible with Morning Prayer.

(3) *Children are periodically present throughout the principal service.* Sometimes when the methods described in the previous paragraph are adopted in the Free Churches they are varied on one Sunday in each month by a service in which the children, except the very youngest, are present throughout, and the term 'Family Service' is then confined to that Sunday. The service must then be simple enough to be intelligible to children and yet serve as the normal principal service for adults. There is some danger that the service may be trivialized; the service may have too bewildering a variety, resembling Babel rather than Pentecost. But the simplicity and directness required by the presence of children may teach valuable lessons for the conduct of services in general. In so far as the service serves as the normal principal service, the best structure is that of the ministry of the word culminating in prayer which is 'eucharistic' in the sense that it is a prayer of thanksgiving. Sometimes indeed the Eucharist itself may be celebrated in full, with the authorized rite of the denomination concerned. But at such services this practice will be rare and will require advance notice and some preparation.

(4) *The Family Service is additional to the principal service.* The term 'Family Service' is also used to mean a service (other than the Eucharist, which was dealt with in para. (1) above) held in addition to and earlier or later than the principal

service; it is usually held every Sunday, but it could be a monthly service. As the Free Churches rarely have two services on a Sunday morning, and Roman Catholics have mostly only Masses, this is largely an Anglican custom, though it is also sometimes found in the Church of Scotland. The Family Service is distinct from the Eucharist and from Morning Prayer. The reason for it is that these are thought to be not simple enough for children; but such Family Services also attract their parents and possibly other adults who are unused to the Eucharist and Morning Prayer. They may thus serve as a bridge over which people may pass from non-attendance at worship to participation in the full worshipping life of the Church, and they provide a good opportunity for evangelistic outreach. The danger is that people may remain for ever on the bridge. Such services must therefore preserve a delicate balance. They need not resemble the Eucharist or Morning Prayer too closely, in so far as they make no claim to be the principal service. Indeed there is no point in providing Family Services in addition to the traditional services unless they are real alternatives affording a real contrast. They may thus be somewhat less tied to traditional shapes and methods than the Free Churches' services described in para. (3) above. On the other hand, they must not diverge too greatly from the traditional shape and style, lest they fail to serve their purpose as a bridge. They may perhaps be described as 'para-liturgical', a category to which other services for other occasions may be added, e.g. civic services.

At Family Services of all these varied kinds, some regard must be had to the main tradition of the Church, e.g. the observance of the Christian year; but there is also need of special guidance and usually of special material suited to their special characters.

QUESTIONS FOR DISCUSSION

1 Which type of Family Service is to be preferred?

2 Are they all appropriate in various settings?

3 What principles and criteria apply to all of them?

4 What special principles and criteria apply to each?

D

12
Special Services

☨

Ronald Jasper

This essay is primarily concerned with those services which are held on single occasions for special groups of people or are connected with some special event. Such services are likely to be attended by a great number of people who do not habitually come to church and for whom the language and the ceremonies used in regular acts of Christian worship may be unfamiliar. Evangelism should therefore be one of their main aims; and it is important that they should be presented in the idiom of those who attend. What will be acceptable to members of the City Guilds in London will not necessarily be acceptable to members of Boys' Clubs in Liverpool.

Two groups of people are normally involved in such services. First there are those who provide the resources and help with the arranging – the clergyman and his staff, the organist, possibly the choir, and members of the regular congregation. These can be regarded as the hosts. Then there are those for whom the service is being provided, and these can be regarded as the guests. The hosts–guests analogy is valuable; for the hosts should make the guests welcome and help them to feel at ease. They should be sensitive to their needs and at all costs should avoid a 'we know what is best for you' attitude. And though these services may be 'one-off' occasions, they can provide opportunity for further – perhaps regular – contact, if the welcome and sensitivity are genuine. Furthermore, if prepared and conducted in the right manner and spirit, they can do much to satisfy those inquirers who may come with an unde-fined and vague sense of hoping for something which they cannot precisely define. They can also do much to direct and deepen the interest of those who are genuinely curious about the Christian faith. Indeed, guests may come to see something of significance and value in their hosts' beliefs and way of life – they may be impressed in some remarkable way.

This does not mean operating what might be called a 'conversion technique'. Hosts can, for example, try to show that Christianity as they understand it is by no means irrelevant to the problems of life or that the Church is not a 'closed shop' of individuals who regard themselves as superior to everyone else. The hosts are not there to overwhelm guests: they are there to help them and to serve them to the best of their ability without appearing in the least condescending; and the guests are left free to make their own decisions and judgements. Nevertheless, hosts have a duty to present a clear and faithful presentation of some aspect of the Christian gospel in the service; and anything less is simply not good enough.

The people who come as guests may have a variety of needs. They may need instruction; they may need to understand how the Church expresses its faith in prayer and worship; they may need to be shown the relevance of the Christian faith to their own particular problems or activities. So the special service should have some theme relevant to the guests involved and it should be brought to a point where it can be seen in the light of the Christian revelation.

Clearly, provision for such services cannot be made effective simply by producing the set forms which are to be found in official prayer books. Nevertheless, with regard to structure the formal services of the Church can help a great deal. Take, for example, the basic structure of the Daily Office or of Ante-Communion in the Anglican form:

> *The Daily Office*
> Introduction
> Psalms
> Lesson
> Canticle
> Lesson
> Canticle
> Prayers

> *Ante-Communion*
> Introduction
> Lesson
> Psalm, Canticle or Hymn
> Lesson
> Psalm, Canticle or Hymn
> Gospel
> Sermon
> Creed and Prayers

Both services have a basic pattern of a series of presentations and responses – a pattern which is one of the earliest in Christian worship and one which can serve our purpose admirably in the construction of a special service. Briefly and simply, what is required is a series of presentations and responses with an introduction and a conclusion.

The introduction should not only make the guests feel welcome, but it should also set before them the theme which undergirds the whole service. Sometimes the theme can arise out of the occasion – a thanksgiving for some particular event or achievement, a commemoration, or even a crisis or an emergency – or it can arise from the needs of the particular group of people who have asked for the service – a school, a civic body, a society or a profession. It is important that the guests should be involved in the preparation of the service. Preliminary consultation can elucidate their particular concerns, which will help in deciding on the theme and will ensure that they really feel that the service is for them and meets their particular needs.

The presentations can take a variety of forms: readings – both scriptural and non-scriptural – tape recordings, music, drama, mime, dance or an address. Equally the response can take different forms – hymns, affirmations, prayers of different kinds – acts of intercession, praise, penitence, thanksgiving and silence. Presentations should also aim to be lucid and related to the needs of those who come, while the responses should encourage the congregation to participate in some way or other. The theme should also be developed logically during the course of the service, and every unit of presentation–response should allow one clear point to be made and acted upon: and because each unit should be fairly short, they should lead on from one another with cumulative effect.

The opening presentation should clearly be concerned with something which is familiar to the guests – the service starts with them – and it might well pose certain questions to which answers can be given in subsequent units of the service. The theme should also be related to the Christian faith, showing, for example, how Jesus Christ supports, or judges, or adds to the experience of the congregation. It is also worth noting that, if we start with something which is familiar, and if most of the congregation are neither committed Christians nor regular churchgoers, great care should be exercised in the selection of material for the first presentation. Something which is non-biblical might well be the best starting point. The Bible can then be introduced later to provide answers to issues which have already been raised.

A service can only be a unity if it moves easily and naturally from one stage to the next. No section of the service, nor the service as a whole, should be overlong. If it is, there is danger that the congregation will become distracted, bored or wearied. The service should also be clearly signposted at every stage, either by clear headings and rubrics in the service paper, or by announcements from the minister, so that the congregation can grasp without difficulty the development of the theme, and the significance of what they themselves are doing at every stage. Finally, the conclusion should do more than merely bring the service to a close, perhaps with a hint or suggestion that this is the end of the matter once and for all. It should encourage or inspire the congregation towards some future policy or line of action, and at the same time it should enable the hosts to indicate that they would welcome further association in the future. A service that starts as a 'one-off' occasion could well become a permanent institution, held annually.

Now for a few comments on particular aspects of special services. First there is the music. It should not necessarily be assumed that all the music used at such services must be 'church music' of the traditional type with organ accompaniment. There is a large and growing number of people today – and especially young people – who can sing or play a variety of instruments. Most of their music is certainly not 'church' music. Some is undeniably poor: but a great deal is not, and this is a resource which should be made use of when suitable opportunity occurs. Some words of the Rev. David Manship are pertinent:

> Modern music in the services is the expression of two ideas, one liturgical, the other theological: first, that it is the people who must share in the act of worship; second, that the common things of life are worth offering. Both these ideas are expressed by the use of community music of an everyday nature, and it has the advantage of securing relevance and involvement . . . The particular properties of much of the modern music – joy, naturalness, full-bloodedness, strength, vigour – are also present in the traditional way, so long as it is presented in an invigorating way.[1]

So when choosing music and its performers, be bold and cast the net as widely as possible.

Secondly, there are the prayers. The prayers can be of different kinds: and silent prayer, set prayer and free prayer are not mutually exclusive. But care and imagination are needed – both in their choice and in their use. Any of them, if used badly or unimaginatively, can be, to quote one writer, 'equally boring and equally repellent'. Silent prayer has not been given its rightful place in public worship, although it now tends to be used much more frequently than some years ago. Silence is something in which all can join, and it can be an effective response to an invitation to pray for some particular cause, or an effective reminder of God's presence. It is also a corporate activity which provides scope for the individual to relate his own particular situation or needs to the theme of the service. But it is a form of prayer which must be used with discretion and in small quantities, especially with people who are not accustomed to it. For them, two minutes of silence in a single dose can seem a very long time.

Of set prayer little needs to be said. Good prayers, well chosen, properly rehearsed and carefully recited can be moving and effective. There may be cases where they may be sufficiently familiar to encourage joint participation. But when badly said and rattled off in long strings, they can be boring and soporific. It is also worth reminding ourselves that some traditional prayers may be familiar enough to a clergyman to be taken for granted, yet to the uninitiated contain language and imagery which mean little.

Free prayer can have the virtues of appropriateness and spontaneity: though again, if badly prepared and executed, it can lack both. Careful preparation is vital, and at all costs we must avoid it becoming verbose, cliché-ridden or appearing to become thinly-disguised sermons. It should be pointed out that the term 'free prayer' is here used in the sense as used by Isaac Watts. For him, free prayer meant prayer which had been prepared beforehand, but was not a set text; whereas extemporary prayer was unprepared and spontaneous, as a spoken response to an unforeseen situation. Nevertheless the two types can be closely allied. The Rev. Wynford Evans has commented: 'Extemporary prayer is like extemporary speaking, since both the speaker and the prayer leader consciously or unconsciously store descriptions, phrases and figures of speech in their mind. With practice they can call them forth at will.'[2]

Those who originally practised free prayer in England were relatively small communities, whose ministers knew their people so well that they could express the things they wished to pray for without difficulty. Moreover, they could assume that members of the congregation knew their Bible. No such personal acquaintance nor such knowledge of the Bible can, however, be assumed at the special services we envisage today. Clichés drawing upon the Bible and high-flown language must therefore be avoided. The minister must pray in terms which are simple and economical, without too much description and amplification. It is not a case of 'keeping God in touch', but of saying sufficient and in such a manner that the congregation can participate intelligently.

Modern prayers do not need to imitate those of the past. We must feel free to explore the modern world with its many realities which unfortunately are so seldom mentioned in prayer – traffic, sanitation, housing, nuclear energy, race relations, and so on. 'They need to stretch out to these realities, and not to avoid dirtying their Sunday suits with them. But with the other hand they need to stretch out to God, and to acknowledge that all the ordinary realities of our lives count with him, and are a part of his single truth.'[3]

Finally, we should remember that if we are to speak meaningfully in services of this kind – whether it be in readings, or prayers, or hymns – it is not enough to use everyday words, even if they are still in use, if all they do is to weave old analogies which lost their significance for urban man at least a hundred years ago. We do not *start* by speaking in terms of shepherds and walled cities to those for whom such terms mean nothing. One is reminded of the comment of the missionary in the Arctic on the difficulty of making an Eskimo understand the significance of the term 'lamb of God'. Nevertheless, there may come a time when such terms can be avoided no longer, for they are there in the Bible, and one of our aims should be that at least some of our guests at special services should come to know and value holy Scripture. But they must be taught to walk before they can run. The preparation of special services is therefore no easy matter, although the benefits derived from them may be supremely worth while.

NOTES

1 John Wilkinson, *Family and Evangelistic Services*, 1967, p. 39.
2 Ibid, p. 47.
3 Ibid, p. 63.

13

Special Occasions
Additions to Basic Forms

✠

A. Raymond George

How are occasional services such as Baptism, Confirmation, Marriage and Ordination to be related to the main or basic services of the Church? In the past they have tended to be separated from the main services, but because of a growing sense of the corporateness of the Church as a family, many of these occasional services are now being more closely linked with the main services.

We must first define the main or principal services. The Eastern Orthodox churches celebrate the Divine Liturgy only once in any one church on any one day, doing so on Sundays and perhaps on some weekdays. Roman Catholic churches usually have several Masses on Sundays and one or more on every weekday – though perhaps fewer now that concelebration is common – as well as parts of the Divine Office. Anglican churches have Morning Prayer, Eucharist and Evening Prayer on Sundays and often on weekdays as well. Sometimes one of these is the best attended, and may be described for our purposes as the principal service.

But in Free Churches and to some extent in the Church of Scotland there are usually only two Sunday services, one in the morning and one in the evening; and though theoretically perhaps these are of equal status, in many places the emphasis is increasingly on the morning. Moreover, with some exceptions such as the Churches of Christ, the Eucharist is not usually celebrated weekly, but more often fortnightly, monthly or quarterly. For the purpose of this chapter we generally describe

81

the Sunday morning service, whether or not a Eucharist, as the principal Sunday service, but we recognize that in some places it is better to regard the Sunday evening service in that way. Such a service is of course also held on certain other days, such as Christmas Day.

The occasional services fall into two main categories, those which conveniently can and those which cannot easily be incorporated into the principal Sunday service. Baptism is a good example of the former; burial, of the latter. Some others, such as ordination, raise further questions.

In the former category we begin with the baptism of infants. It used to be held very often on Sunday afternoons, either during Sunday school or after Sunday school (with a congregation drawn from such teachers and scholars as were willing to stay) or entirely detached from the Sunday school, the congregation consisting almost entirely of the family and friends of the child. Now baptisms have largely moved into the morning service, not only because of the decline of afternoon Sunday schools but, more importantly, because of the growing sense of the corporate significance of baptism. This shift has unfortunately encountered some resistance because it slightly lengthens the service and, if frequent, is sometimes felt to be monotonous. Indeed it might even be said that the incorporation of baptisms in the principal service is a luxury which the English Free Churches can allow themselves because they do not usually have too many baptisms to cope with. If they are numerous, attempts are often made to gather them on one Sunday in the month. Certainly this incorporation is to be encouraged.

In general, occasional services incorporated in the principal service come after the lessons and sermon, which is appropriate as they are a response to the proclamation. Baptism is often an exception. This is usually on the ground that the children will profit by being present at it, and that it must be done before they depart for their lessons. It might also be defended on the ground that baptism is an entry to the Church's worship and thus might well stand at the beginning of it. This argument is not, however, very sound. The baptism of adults in the early Church occurred *after* they had long taken part in the Word-service as catechumens, and the baptism of infants occurs today only because their parents are responding to the message of Scripture, heard, of course, on earlier occasions but symbolically represented by the lessons of that service. It might be possible to welcome the infants and their parents at the beginning of the service, but to keep the baptism till after the sermon; the parents and their friends would thus hear the sermon, but the infants could be taken out for a while. The children of the Junior Church could come back for this. In any case the sermon usually comes earlier in the service than it used to do; it is followed by the concluding prayers of the service, which may well incorporate thanksgiving and petition appropriate to the occasion, or by the communion. Most service-books for the most part incorporate rubrics pointing in these directions, though allowing in some cases a certain flexibility. The question arises what lessons are appropriate. Here flexibility is definitely required. Some passage or passages relating to baptism should always be read as a warrant for the service. But in addition to these some or all of the lessons for the Sunday should usually also be read, especially on major festivals such as Easter Day. But on occasion, not too frequently, the whole service may take baptism as its theme, in which case all the readings should be directly or indirectly about baptism. Some of the service-books make provision accordingly.

Believers' baptism is such a major occasion in Baptist churches and in the Churches of Christ that it is naturally done at the principal service (sometimes held in the evening), which is built around it. The same is true in paedo-baptist churches of Confirmation or Reception into Full Membership or Admission to Holy Communion. The lessons will usually be chosen for the occasion, the confirmation will come after the sermon (which will be a 'charge' to the candidates), and the service will culminate in Holy Communion, though in Anglican churches this has not in the past been very common. In Anglican churches the need for the presence of a bishop means that the confirmation is often done at a special service on a weekday. On the comparatively rare occasions when in paedo-baptist churches baptism is administered to those who are able to answer for themselves, this is usually done at the same service as the confirmation, though sometimes the shyness of the candidate leads to it being done 'privately' a day or so before the confirmation.

There are, however, other services connected with the birth of children: thanksgiving for the birth or the adoption of a child;

83

presentation, blessing and dedication of children, and dedication of parents. In the Prayer Book there is a service called 'The Thanksgiving of Women after Child-Birth commonly called The Churching of Women'; the rubrics refer to the possibility that it may precede the Communion. It was usually said in private on a weekday, sometimes through a superstitious belief that ill-luck would be incurred if the woman did anything else before she was 'churched'; now it seems sensible to include a brief service of thanksgiving for the birth of a child in the principal service or simply to mention the birth among the subjects for thanksgiving in the prayers of the principal service; but many would think that the joyful baptism of the infant is sufficient in itself. Thanksgiving after adoption is somewhat similar, but if the adopted child has already been baptised it may be thought appropriate to have this additional ceremony to mark his or her entry into a new family.

Services for the presentation, blessing and/or dedication of children and/or dedication of parents are a different matter. They are not of course baptism, but in churches which do not practise infant baptism services with such names as these serve as a ceremony to mark the birth of a child; it is, of course, hoped that the child will eventually seek baptism as a believer. It seems best to incorporate them into the principal service. Such services sometimes serve the same purpose for committed and practising members of paedo-baptist churches who prefer not to have their children baptized. Some ministers of paedo-baptist churches indeed encourage this alternative procedure for non-committed and non-practising parents, but if the parents are not sufficiently committed or practising Christians to take the promises involved in infant baptism, they can hardly be expected to take the promises involved in any kind of dedication, though they might desire a service of blessing. Paedo-baptist churches usually refrain from authorizing official services of presentation, dedication or blessing lest they seem to be weakening in their attachment to paedo-baptist views. When, however, such services are unofficially composed, they may also include the theme of thanksgiving for the birth. Sometimes indeed a service of thanksgiving for the birth, despite its origin as additional to infant baptism, is itself used as the main ceremony marking the birth of a child where infant baptism is not desired.

The other 'rites of passage', marriage and funerals, fall into the category of rites which one cannot easily fit into the principal Sunday service, so that it is doubtful whether it is even theoretically desirable to attempt to do so, though it might be possible to include a brief blessing of a civil marriage. There are three ways in which a marriage may be linked with the principal Sunday service without forming a part of it. The first is indicated in the new *Book of Common Order* (1979) of the Church of Scotland:

> A marriage service is an event in the life of the Church. At that service the Church does three things. She resumes her worship at the high point reached on the Lord's Day, the point of thanksgiving, and now relates the thanksgiving to the special happiness of the marriage day: she turns again gratefully to the word, i.e. scripture, read and sometimes briefly preached: in the buoyancy of faith she prays and blesses the couple from God.

On that view it is not appropriate to include Holy Communion, and it is often thought to be inappropriate also on the ground that the special 'mixed' congregation at a wedding is likely to include some who are not normally communicants.

The second way is to celebrate the marriage within a nuptial Mass or Communion service, usually on a weekday. It comes, like most such ceremonies, most conveniently between the Ministry of the Word (which acts as a kind of warrant) and the Lord's Supper. Another way is to put the declaration of purpose and the legal declarations before the collect and the lessons and the marriage after. The sermon or address may either follow the lessons immediately or come after the marriage, in which case it becomes the first preaching of the word to the newly-married couple. These are probably better methods than simply having the marriage first, followed by the Ministry of the Word and the Lord's Supper. In any of these patterns the communion is sometimes restricted to the officiating ministers and the bridal couple, but it is probably better for it to be open to all who would normally receive it.

The third way, which is really an adaptation of the second, is to celebrate the marriage within a service which, while not the principal Sunday service, has to some extent the same shape, but without communion. The same variations are possible as regards the relation of the parts of the marriage to the Ministry of the Word, and the Lord's Supper is replaced by a concluding prayer of thanksgiving (a kind of 'dry' anaphora), a principle which applies to other services also.

Funerals do not fit into the principal Sunday service, nor is their traditional shape 'eucharistic', the customary psalms, readings and prayers in Anglican and many other churches are distantly descended from the office for the dead, though even here a note of thanksgiving at the end of the service may strike a 'eucharistic' note. In the Roman Catholic Church, however, the funeral service normally takes the form of a Requiem Mass, preceded perhaps by a service at the house and the reception of the body into the church. The final commendation and farewell follow the Mass, and then comes the interment at a cemetery. Anglicans similarly sometimes combine the funeral service with the communion service in various ways. The Church of Scotland and the Free Churches have naturally no equivalent of a Requiem Mass; that is to say, they hardly ever have a special celebration of the Holy Communion in connection with a funeral. But a link may be made with the Sunday service by making appropriate reference at the principal service on the following Sunday; sometimes indeed the family mourners attend that, and it almost assumes the form of a memorial service; but this custom is dying out.

Ordinations are in some churches held only on Sundays or other holy days, but in others ordinations (and in most churches inductions) are usually done on weekdays, but such a service resembles a principal Sunday service in that it is attended by the whole normal congregation as well as special guests. The lessons of course fit the occasion, and a sermon and/or a charge (a word used by different churches in different senses) may be put in various places. The same problems arise about Holy Communion as at a marriage: is it appropriate in a 'mixed' congregation? Is it practicable for a large number of people to communicate? But the congregation, while containing some special guests, is more likely to consist of regular communicants than at a marriage, and it is very appropriate that entry on the ministry of word and sacrament should be marked by a celebration of the sacrament of the Lord's Supper. Indeed some would think it appropriate that at an ordination the newly-ordained minister(s) should concelebrate with the presiding minister, and that at an induction the newly-inducted minister should then preside at the Lord's Supper. These practices, however, are not yet widespread.

There are, of course, many other services: commissioning (in some cases ordination) of elders, deacons, deaconesses, lay or local preachers, leaders, Sunday school teachers and workers among young people; opening and dedication of churches, dedication of items of church furniture and of Scout and Guide flags; also special kinds of service at particular seasons – toy services, carol services, christingle services and Mothering Sunday services. Of these it may be said that a major occasion, such as the opening of a church, calls for a full service in the style of a principal service to be held usually on a weekday; commissionings and dedications of people are often done similarly; smaller occasions, such as the dedication of a Scout flag, are best done after the sermon at the Sunday service; very few of these are done 'privately'. Occasions like Mothering Sunday demand a choice: either the principal service is somewhat adapted to the occasion or a special service is held at some other time.

There are also the more traditional observances which mark the Christian year: the midnight communion at Christmas, the watchnight, the Methodist covenant service, the ceremonies of Ash Wednesday, and above all those of Holy Week and Easter. For the last, the Roman Catholic Church prescribes forms, and the Episcopal Church in Scotland has published *Services and Ceremonies for Ash Wednesday and Holy Week* authorized for permissive use in 1967. Unofficial forms have circulated fairly widely in the Church of England, but the use of such forms has not been extensive in the Church of Scotland and the English Free Churches, though special services on Maundy Thursday and Good Friday are common. The Joint Liturgical Group has already published its adaptations of them in *Holy Week Services* (ed. R. C. D. Jasper, 1971).

Another form of addition to the principal service lies in the agape or love-feast. This practice of the early Church had died out till it was revived by Moravians and Methodists. It had almost, though not quite, died out again, till it was again revived, partly as an ecumenical occasion where inter-communion is not possible. Sometimes, indeed, with doubtful honesty, it is observed in such a form that it is scarcely dis-tinguishable from the Lord's Supper, so that those who wish may regard it as such and those whose Churches do not permit intercommunion may regard it as simply a fellowship-meal. But, quite apart from that, the widespread, particularly Anglican, custom of the parish breakfast following parish communion pre-serves many of the values of the agape. Another variant is the extended communion, in which the specifically eucharistic acts are done in the setting of a full meal. Sometimes also simple observances added to a domestic meal turn it into a kind of agape, in which children can easily take part.

All these varied observances have their own style and validity; yet to see all as linked in some way with the principal service of the Church and in particular with the eucharist is a way of ensur-ing that they are rooted in the central theme of the gospel, Jesus Christ crucified and risen.

QUESTIONS FOR DISCUSSION

1 Which of the occasional services are best incorporated into the principal service, and at what point?

2 How are those which are not incorporated into the principal service to be linked with it?

14

Appendix

Report of a Workshop on the Worship of the Congregation

The Orthodox Academy, Gonia/Chania, Crete
8 – 15 April 1978

☩

World Council of Churches
Sub-unit on Renewal and Congregational Life

Worship is not new to the ecumenical agenda.

The two central acts of Christian worship – baptism and the Eucharist – have been focal points for discussion between the churches since the earliest days of the modern ecumenical movement. There have been other approaches to the issue too, notably the section of the World Council's Uppsala Assembly (1968) that worked on 'Worship in a Secular Age' and a workshop at the succeeding Nairobi Assembly (1975) that tackled 'Spirituality'.

Less formally, liturgical developments during the past thirty years have crossed denominational frontiers with remarkable ease so that there are clear affinities between what is happening in, say, Roman Catholic congregations in Ghana and those of the United Presbyterian Church in the USA. Ecumenical structures, especially in recent years, have provided venues for liturgical creativity: for example, when the Christian Conference of Asia sponsored the publication of *Christian Art in Asia*, the World Council produced a new edition of the multi-lingual, multi-cultural, multi-denominational hymnal *Cantate Domino*, and the Nairobi Assembly prepared prayers and songs as vehicles for conveying its insights to the churches.

The concern, then, has not been forgotten. But it may be asked whether worship has been given attention proportionate to its central importance for the day-by-day, year-by-year life of the churches.

Then came the Nairobi Assembly's call for the World Council to respond more directly to the needs, problems and possibilities of local congregations. Translating this into programme, the newly-created WCC Sub-unit on Renewal and Congregational Life identified 'The Worship of the Congregation' as one area to be explored to see how churches might find ways of assisting each other's efforts towards renewal.

That was how twenty-five people, from all major Christian traditions and many parts of the world, found themselves at the Orthodox Academy, Crete, in April 1978. Some were experts in the history of Christian worship, some were responsible for liturgical commissions in their own churches, some were pastors, some musicians and poets, some social activists, some teachers of theology. All came as individuals, not official delegates of churches. What the very disparate group had in common was a shared conviction that what happens in a congregation's corporate worship is of crucial importance for every other aspect of its life and witness.

Participants began with short reports on the present state of congregational worship in their respective churches. Some striking similarities emerged – for example, the widespread rediscovery of the centrality of the Eucharist. Some clear disagreements were identified – e.g. on the relation of worship to culture. Some issues surfaced but were not explored, e.g. the significance of liturgical life for children, and vice versa. Throughout, the workshop was acutely aware of the Orthodox setting in which it met.

What follows is a collation of insights that emerged, disagreements that remained, and suggestions that are directed to the churches and the WCC for taking the exploration further. Such exploration, the report notes, 'demands of us all an openness to Christians of other confessions, times, cultures and ideologies, as well as a willingness to contribute to the quest of other Christians as they for their part engage in the same pilgrimage of faith.' Sharing among Christians can be disturbing. It can also, the workshop participants gratefully testify, be profoundly enriching.

David M. Gill

Worship: What it is, What it is not

1 'Liturgy' means literally 'the work of the people'. In classical Greek the word was used to describe the contribution an individual made to some corporate or public enterprise. The Church took over this term and enriched its meaning. The New Testament uses it to describe one's service to God (e.g. Zechariah performing his priestly functions in the Temple) and also one's service to a neighbour. Significantly, it is also used to describe the high-priestly, sacrificial function of Jesus Christ which is a self-offering directed at once towards both God and humanity.[1]

2 Jesus himself, through his death, resurrection and ascension, brings into being a new temple, a creation no longer of wood and stone but of flesh and blood – a building of living stones, with himself as the foundation and indwelt by the Holy Spirit. The new temple is the Body of Christ, and wherever one encounters another in the power of the Spirit of the risen Christ, there true worship takes place. In the vision of the new Jerusalem, no temple was necessary.

3 Clearly the New Testament sees worship in this dual sense – service directed both to God and to humanity (e.g. Rom. 12). The early Church saw no real dichotomy between worship, work and witness. Worship and living the Christian life were two aspects of one total activity. Their unity, today, needs urgently to be recovered.

4 Christ is the heart of the Church, and the Eucharist the central act of the Church. He invites all men and women to come to his table. By his Word and Spirit, Jesus Christ is present in his divinity and humanity, his humiliation and exaltation as the perfect sacrifice of God made once and for all. As the steward of the Eucharist the Church proclaims most perfectly through the Holy Spirit what it is: a eucharistic community. As the people of God eat the bread and drink the cup

they are thankful for the reconciliation which occurs in Jesus Christ. They are nourished as God's agents with a ministry to the world in word and deed. As they remember Christ's sacrifice they are 're-membered' as brothers and sisters who love God and serve their neighbour, re-affirming the unity of their baptism and re-committing themselves in all their diversity to participate in Christ's mission in the world. They are leaven through which Christ in the Spirit transforms society, the people themselves being renewed in each creative and faithful celebration of the Eucharist, and thus a foretaste of what is to come in the final consummation.

5 With the WCC's Faith and Order Commission, we have noted the remarkable revaluing of the central significance of the Eucharist at present taking place within many churches.[2] It must be underlined, however, that inherent in the notion of a eucharistic community is the understanding of this community as committed to the transformation of society. For as the Orthodox Consultation on 'Confessing Christ through the Liturgical Life of the Church Today' stated:

> The Liturgy is not an escape from life, but a continuous transformation of life according to the prototype Jesus Christ, through the power of the Spirit.

And again:

> The liturgy has to be continued in personal everyday situations. Every one of the faithful is called upon to continue a secret devotion, on the secret altar of his own heart, to realize a living proclamation of the good news 'for the sake of the whole world'. Without this continuation the liturgy remains half finished . . . Since the liturgy is the participation in the great Event of liberation from the demonic powers, then the continuation of liturgy in life means a continuous liberation from the powers of the evil that are working inside us (e.g. the terrible complex of egoism), a continual re-orientation and openness to insights and efforts aiming at liberating human persons from all demonic structures of injustice, exploitation, agony, loneliness, and aiming at creating real communion of persons in love.[3]

Faithfulness and Creativity

6 The people of God are called to a life of creative faithfulness. Their faithfulness is in the first place to their Lord, made known in holy Scripture. He is the same yesterday, today and for ever. Yet he also goes before, summoning us to share with him in the shaping of the future.

7 The people of God are called to be faithful to the *living* tradition of the Church. By emphasizing the word 'living' we remind each other that tradition does not merely equal the past and is therefore not a static possession. In the power (*dynamis*) of the Holy Spirit tradition is dynamic precisely because at the heart of it is the process of 'handing on' Christ to successive generations, with all the risks that involves. In a sense, the Church's mission requires that it live simultaneously at the end, in the midst and at the beginning of this tradition.

8 Faithfulness to tradition requires therefore the utmost sensitivity – to the claims of God who does not change, and to the needs of men and women who are always changing. To be faithfully creative and creatively faithful we must be renewed constantly, individually and corporately, in commitment to our unchanging Lord and to the ever-changing world that is the object of his saving love.

9 Human creativeness can only be a reflection of the creativity of God. It draws upon what has already been made available by God, for example, culture, art, material things, words, music. The people of God are called to see such things through the eyes of Christ. Only so can the Church responsibly re-examine its worship, fully using all the gifts with which God has endowed us and alert to the endless possibilities he puts before us.

Worship and Culture

10 The gospel is both universal and particular. It preaches Jesus of one time and place to people of every age and nation. In principle, there need be no conflict between the universal character of the gospel and its particular character. In fact, however, the preaching of the message raises delicate problems of translation as the attempt is made to find an expression which is both faithful to the original and yet intelligible in a

different culture from that of Jesus. Such efforts risk presenting the gospel in forms that other Christians cannot regard as true expressions of the faith. There is need therefore to discern a universal norm, and to respect legitimate variety of expression.

11 Stated most simply, the *universal norm* of Christianity is Jesus Christ. As far as worship is concerned, Christian liturgy is taking place when it is possible to discern Jesus Christ in the reading and exposition of the Scriptures, which bear earliest witness to him; when prayers are being made 'in his name'; when his sacramental presence is experienced; and when he is seen in the quality of life displayed by the worshippers also beyond the special moments of the cult. The discernment of Jesus Christ under these aspects is not without its problems: scriptural exegesis and interpretation is involved, with the danger of error on the part of scholar and preacher; prayer which is truly 'in the name of Christ' demands the schooling of discipleship; the sacramental presence of Jesus Christ has been the subject of dispute among Christians; attempts to 'follow Christ' in ethical behaviour always take place within the limits of particular circumstances.

12 Diverse *particular forms* are shaped by many factors. culture changes with time. There is also at any one time a great mixture of different peoples with different cultures, and these interact with one another. This variety and interaction take place within the context of a common humanity. As a witness to God who is both the beginning and end of humanity, the Church of Jesus Christ will guard and affirm all that is positive in a culture; it will challenge and criticize all that runs counter to God's design.

13 The particular elements and peculiar expressions of liturgy are a necessary consideration in the quest for liturgical renewal. The New Testament itself translated Semitic forms into Hellenistic expressions as Christianity was spread to the Greeks. The means adopted by Peter and Paul to present Christ to Jews and Gentiles showed variety and cultural adaptations (e.g. Acts 17). Furthermore, modern scholars have detected hymns of the early Church's liturgical celebrations which stem from Hellenistic congregations (e.g. Col. 1.15–20; Phil. 2.5–11).

14 Thus cultural adaptation is canonized by its presence in

Scripture. The biblical model sets such translation as a permanent task for every generation in every culture. There is also the accepted truth that God is universal Creator, and created people of differing cultures are meant to have multiple characteristics. Furthermore, the incarnation of Jesus Christ is the supreme expression of the need to become incarnational in our respective settings.

15 *Symbols* provide an illustration of the importance of cultural diversity for liturgical renewal. There are universally accepted archetypes, e.g. eating together, greetings, motherhood, light, which are related to everyday life. They are living aids that speak profoundly to men and women in their own situations. When used in liturgy, these symbols normally serve the sense of the divine presence. These archetypes are manifested in various symbolic forms in various cultures, for human beings are symbol-making creatures. Liturgy cannot exist without symbols, and a rediscovery of the place and use of symbols is a necessary ingredient in liturgical renewal.

16 Symbols generally involve the whole person with *all* his/her senses. Churches which shape their worship solely for the ear or even for the intellect alone need to recover an appreciation of all the aesthetic senses. For example:

(*a*) The recurrent tendency to portray Christ and the biblical scenes in terms of the artist's own culture should be encouraged.

(*b*) For many centuries some churches have known the value of the icon as a visible means of contact with the hidden reality it represents, and other churches could well learn from this.

(*c*) With music, men and women express themselves in ways which people of other cultures also can appreciate – consider, for example, the widespread use of spirituals that originated with blacks in North America. Moreover, music is never purely a matter for the ear alone; it engages by its rhythm the whole person.

(*d*) In liturgy, processions, gestures and other bodily postures are viewed as vivid symbols conveying spiritual meanings. For example, forms of salutation vary from country to country, yet they carry with them the meaning of mutual acceptance, peace and blessing.

(*e*) Dress has always been a way in which people of a particular time and place express their identity. Individuals fulfilling liturgical functions have usually been distinguished by special vestments, and churches should reflect carefully on the meaning conveyed by such symbols.

Worship and Social Engagement

17 Liturgical renewal requires a recovery of the unity of worship and life, the integrity of cultic celebration with 'the daily liturgy of the faithful' that should be expressed by it and follow from it. A community that is truly eucharistic follows its Lord in offering its life for the life of the world.

18 Such self-giving may take many forms, according to the situation in which a congregation finds itself. It may include political involvement with the oppressed and/or compassionate service to the needy. It will, in every case, entail lifting up specific concerns for the suffering in the prayers of the faithful. Indeed, in places where freedoms are severely curtailed, the liturgy itself with its celebration of One who proclaimed good news to the poor and liberty to the captives becomes itself a daring political act.

19 Yet in too many situations there remains a wide gap between the radical proclamation of salvation and liberation that occurs in Christian liturgies, on the one hand, and the way the Christian community lives and witnesses in society, on the other. There are some obvious reasons for this:

(*a*) The Church is an institution caught up in the attitudes, structures and political pressures of the society in which it is set.

(*b*) Social engagement by churches or individuals may be feared as likely to spark controversy and threaten the cohesiveness of the congregation.

(*c*) It is not easy for those parts of the Church that are encumbered with wealth to become signs and servants of Christ 'who for our sakes became poor'.

20 These factors have received considerable attention in recent ecumenical thought. There is, however, another reason for the gap – one that has been the particular concern of this workshop. For many, the liturgy – be it 'new' or 'old' – is often lacking in personal significance for the worshipper and offers insufficient scope for meaningful participation by the congregation. When the congregation itself has a role in preparing and conducting its worship, the liturgy may become a more effective means for all concerned to identify more fully with its significance for their own lives. But the problem goes deeper yet.

21 The real crisis in the Church that inhibits Christian social engagement is a matter not so much of liturgical renewal as of renewal of the spirit. Are the hearts and minds of the faithful attuned to the proclamations, the judgements and the promises of the liturgy? The worship and witness of a congregation come alive when its members are alive to God and to one another. To be able to see Christ in each other is to be able to see him in all people everywhere. To live intensely with God is to live intensely with the neighbour in the congregation, in the local community, in the world at large.

22 This in turn leads to other questions the workshop was unable to explore in any depth. Are not our pastors themselves, under the many pressures of their work, often in need of spiritual renewal? Does the charismatic renewal movement have a significant word to say to us all? How does the quest for visible unity among Christians relate to this need for renewal?

23 The process of liturgical revision now under way in many churches clearly is to be welcomed and encouraged. Equally clearly, such revision in itself is no guarantee that our congregations will become more compassionate and courageous in their social engagement. Our liturgies set forth the good news of salvation and liberation. The issue is whether the churches are prepared at all levels of their life to respond to the radical challenges those liturgies place before us.

Some Questions and Recommendations

24 *True worship*, Paul makes clear in his letter to the Romans (12.1), entails offering ourselves 'as a living sacrifice to God, dedicated to his service and pleasing to him'. As God's great mercy to us embraces the whole of life, so too the whole of life

must be caught up in our response. The focal point of this response is the eucharistic celebration of Christ's people gathered in each place in the name of their crucified and risen Lord. The very dynamics of the celebration demand, however, that it never be divorced from the totality of the 'living sacrifice' that centres upon it.

Why is this link between liturgy and life not more maintained in our congregations? What are the spiritual disciplines necessary for effective work and witness? Some Christians, while regularly involved in liturgical acts, seem to find it difficult to translate this involvement into compassionate action for justice and peace. An order of worship might say all the right things but somehow does not work itself out in the life of the community. Others, while deeply committed to responding to human need, seem to see little significance in liturgical celebration. Are there ways in which the churches can help one another towards a liturgical life and obedience more expressive of 'true worship'?

25 Our efforts towards liturgical renewal find their point of reference in *the common source* of all Christian worship – that is, the Christ-event as confessed and celebrated by the Spirit-filled community that is the Church (cf. 1 Cor. 11.23ff). The Tradition 'received from the Lord' is now received in all our churches under the conditions of historically and culturally determined traditions and today, as in every age, it must be allowed to speak its word afresh. Renewal in worship requires that we seek to discern more clearly the Tradition, within and beyond our several traditions, that comes truly from the Lord. Such a search is difficult. It is disturbing. It demands of us all an openness to Christians of other confessions, times, cultures and ideologies, as well as a willingness to contribute to the quest of other Christians as they for their part engage in the same pilgrimage of faith. This way of obedience is also the way of renewal and unity – as recent Faith and Order work towards a consensus on the Eucharist clearly exemplifies.

All our churches are wedded to traditions – modern, ancient or both. Of some we are conscious, of others we may not even be aware. At no point do these become more evident than in our worship. Are there ways the churches can help one another identify, explore and evaluate their respective liturgical traditions in this quest for the Tradition? Can we find ways of sustaining one another through the disturbance this entails?

26 Fidelity to the Tradition requires continuing creativity as we seek, in changing human contexts, to understand the incomprehensible, to express the inexpressible, to celebrate the great and glorious mystery of the gospel. Today, as in every age, our liturgies should draw extensively and confidently on the *symbolic resources of our various cultures*. Liturgy demands the participation of the whole person and all his or her faculties. It requires the active involvement of the whole congregation, not least in the quest for symbols that for its people will be bearers of the mystery. It points to the need for continuing mutual support and questioning of the churches one of another, to stimulate, share and correct their creative endeavours. There is, of course, a danger of distortion inherent in every quest for cultural symbols – ancient or modern, in 'Christian' societies no less than those shaped by other religions – but fidelity itself requires a readiness to risk creativity.

A sense of the numinous is a vital aspect of Christian worship. How can we discover or recover it? Are our congregations drawing the whole person (mind, vision, physical responsiveness, etc.) into their liturgical events? Are they in fact giving fullest possible expression to the gifts (charisms) of their members, for example, in the preparation of acts of worship? How do they manifest this search for contemporary symbols, and in what ways in this regard are they open to the critical questioning of churches in other times and places? This in turn raises the question for each church: how does it understand its relation to culture (as guardian, critic, transformer or what?) and are there certain unexamined assumptions about the relation between church and culture that may need review?

27 Each congregation of Christ's people lives and celebrates in the midst of a *concrete socio-political situation*. It can be neither faithful nor creative without wrestling with the question of what Christ in that situation requires of it. There is a twofold

temptation: (*a*) that of celebrating in a 'sacred world' that is cut off from the cries and needs of people; and (*b*) that of an activism or a partisanship that subordinates the proclamation of the paschal mystery to political ends. There is, however, a partisanship that must find expression in the Church's worship as in the totality of its life and witness, for it is the partisanship of God himself towards the poor, the oppressed, the forgotten. Neutrality on this point is impossible. Consequent tensions, between Church and society and within the churches themselves, are inevitable. The poor themselves are part of the test of all our attempts at fidelity and creativity, in liturgy or in anything else.

How are particular ideological assumptions and political commitments, explicit or implicit, reflected in the liturgies of our churches? Are there ways we can help each other assess which of these may be valid, which invalid? What is the role of the marginalized of any society in shaping the worship of the congregation? In some situations of acute societal problems the liturgy does not engender social-political involvement. Is this because liturgy itself is irrelevant or because the people's response is inadequate? What problems are raised for liturgical planning by diverging political convictions within congregations, and how may these be dealt with?

28 In addition to the general reflections and questions raised above, we offer a number of *concrete suggestions*:

(*a*) In regular acts of worship, following traditional patterns and local usages, those responsible should take careful account of the various essential elements and make these elements accessible to the congregations.

(*b*) 'Free space' should be created for testing and improving upon both traditional and contemporary elements of liturgical practice. Groups of young people, families, housechurches, vacation groups and special feasts of the whole congregation provide natural settings for such testing.

(*c*) New ecumenical contacts provide opportunities for congregations to experience the inner meaning of other liturgical traditions, and may thereby open the way for a greater creativity within each tradition.

29 It is important for the liturgical witness of the Church that the churches should agree upon a *unified calendar* without delay, to enable Christians to celebrate together the mysteries of Christ's birth and resurrection. We urge our churches, with the assistance of the World Council of Churches, to press ahead for an early resolution to this problem.

30 Current developments concerning the Eucharist lead us to propose that the World Council take further steps to help the churches give *liturgical expression to their emerging doctrinal agreement*. Specifically, we recommend the preparation of one or more liturgical structures that accord with the consensus already achieved, to be offered to the churches as contributions to their own efforts at liturgical revision and for possible use as 'approved alternatives' to existing denominational forms. Further, in view of the work now being done in several places to prepare alternative ecumenical texts for the eucharistic canon, it is proposed that the WCC seek to make such texts as well as other material for worship more widely available for use as desired by the churches.

31 The experience of this workshop convinces us of the value of such exchanges of liturgical insights and experience, traditional as well as contemporary, to grasp the points of growing convergence, discern possibilities for mutual enrichment and clarify sources of continuing disagreement. To be most fruitful, however, such encounters must take full account of the cultural contexts in which particular churches find themselves. We recommend, therefore, that the WCC initiate *a three-year project of regional worship workshops*, possibly concluding with a worldwide evaluation meeting prior to the next WCC Assembly. Specific suggestions for the possible duration, composition and style of such workshops have been conveyed to the staff. It is our conviction that these encounters, building wherever possible on efforts already under way in the regions, would multiply naturally once their value was experienced. This is a concrete way in which the World Council of Churches could help the churches help one another towards the renewal of the worship of our congregations.

PARTICIPANTS

The Rev. John Ambrose, United Church of Canada

The Rev. Patrick A. B. Anthony, Director, Folk Research Centre, St Lucia, West Indies

Mr Athanasios Apostolou, Orthodox Academy of Crete

The Rev. Elias Audi, Athens

The Rev. Dr A. W. Godfrey Brown, Presbyterian Church of Ireland

The Rev. Canon Lloyd S. Casson, Washington Cathedral, USA

The Rev. Canon Rex Davis, The Subdeanery, Lincoln

Bishop Dometian, Sofia, Bulgaria

The Rev. John Gatu, Presbyterian Church of East Africa, Kenya

Metropolitan Irineos, Holy Metropolis Chania, Crete

The Very Rev. Ronald Jasper, The Deanery, York

Mr Elias Jones, Geneva

The Rev. Fred Kaan, United Reformed Church, England

The Venerable Samir Kafity, Episcopal Church in Jerusalem and the Middle East

The Rev. Dr James G. Kirk, United Presbyterian Church in the USA

The Rev. Per Larsson, Church of Sweden

The Rev. Paul Lebeau, SJ, Lumen Vitae, Brussels

The Rev. Lydia N. Niguidula, Silliman University, Philippines

The Rev. Dr Paul P. Park, Methodist Theological Seminary, Seoul, Korea

Miss Martha Roy, Cairo, Egypt

Dr Reinhild Traitler, World Council of Churches, Geneva

Propst Dieter Trautwein, Lutheran Church, Federal Republic of Germany

Dr Geoffrey Wainwright, Queen's College, Birmingham

The Rev. David Gill, World Council of Churches, Geneva

NOTES

1 The following biblical references show the various dimensions of the New Testament usage of the word 'liturgy': priestly offering to God in worship: Luke 1.23; Hebrews 9.21; 10.11; Christ's heavenly priesthood: Hebrews 8.2; 8.6; service to people: 2 Corinthians 9.12; Philippians 2.30; Romans 13.6; 15.27; the Christian's life as a sacrifice: Philippians 2.17; proclaiming God's Gospel: Romans 15.16.

2 See *One Baptism, One Eucharist and a Mutually Recognized Ministry: Three Agreed Statements* (Faith and Order paper No. 73); and the subsequent *A Response to the Churches* (Faith and Order paper No. 84), pp. 8–9.

3 International Review of Mission, October 1975, pp. 420–1.